Unbelievable!

Also co-authored by Myan Subrayan
Inga: My Story with Inga Tuigamala
More than Rugby with Pierre Spies

Chad le Clos
Unbelievable!

with Myan Subrayan

PENGUIN BOOKS

First published by Penguin Books (South Africa) (Pty) Ltd, 2014
A Penguin Random House company
Registered Offices: Block D, Rosebank Office Park, 181 Jan Smuts Avenue, Parktown
North, Johannesburg 2193, South Africa

www.penguinbooks.co.za

ISBN 978-0-14-353865-3
eISBN 978-0-14-353127-2

Text design and typesetting by Triexie Smit in 10.5/14pt NewsGoth
Cover design by mr design
Cover photograph by Chris Allan
Printed and bound by CTP Printers, Cape Town

To the youth of South Africa:
Be inspired to know that dreams can come true, so keep
dreaming and make sure you work hard to achieve them.
Remember, the only place where 'success' comes
before 'work' is in the dictionary!

Contents

Foreword by Sam Ramsamy

On the last day of July 2012, Chad le Clos became the darling of the swimming world.

Michael Phelps of the US was then the world swimming icon. It seemed highly unlikely that anyone would be able to beat him in a butterfly event at the Olympic Games. Phelps was tipped to win both the 100 m and 200 m butterfly at the 2012 Olympic Games in London. Chad le Clos felt privileged to be drawn to swim in the lane next to Phelps, his role model and idol, for the 200 m butterfly final. The result astounded Phelps: he was beaten by the then 20-year-old South African. It was sheer joy for South Africa. Chad's parents, Geraldine and Bert, had been watching the race from near me. Bert hugged me tightly. I could feel that he was perspiring profusely from his great excitement. With all our emotions running high, I too was overwhelmed, but I needed to collect myself to present the gold medal to Chad.

I realised the presentation brief for the medal ceremony was beckoning, but we simply had to celebrate immediately, so I quickly made my way to the VIP hospitality arena, grabbed some bottles of beer, handed them to Bert and rushed to the presentation area for the official briefing on the ceremony.

Another race was under way before the presentation of the medals for the 200 m butterfly would take place. Then Chad arrived. He must have spent some time recovering in the changing room after his extraordinary victory, I thought, because he looked so calm and composed. That presentation ceremony belonged in every sense to South Africa – Chad stood on the victory podium; the South African flag was hoisted; the national anthem was played.

A few days later, Chad was in the final of the 100 m butterfly. After the first 50 m, he was nowhere near achieving a medal. Then he put on a superb sprint and he nearly did it again. This time, he finished second.

Having been the founding president of Swimming South Africa (SSA) – I am now its honorary life president – and the founding president of the National Olympic Committee of South Africa, I always make South African swimming a high priority of mine. I had seen the rise of another

South African swimming sensation, Penny Heyns, who won the double breaststroke events at the 1996 Olympic Games in Atlanta.

And I have been following the untiring efforts of Chad's coach, Graham Hill, one of South Africa's foremost swimming coaches. Graham's dedication had been evident at the Sydney Olympic Games in 2000, when one of his charges, Terence Parkin, won a silver medal. The Parkin–Hill combination was an extraordinary feat, considering that Terence is deaf. Chad was greatly inspired by Terence's achievement and wanted to emulate his success.

I closely follow the swimmers Graham coaches, so when Chad performed exceptionally at the 2010 Youth Olympic Games in Singapore, I knew we had a potential medallist for the 2012 Games.

As a member of the International Olympic Committee (IOC), I have the honour of presenting medals to the Olympic winners. After discussing the issue with Graham, I decided I would present the medals for the men's 100 m breaststroke and 200 m butterfly. Chad complimented me for having chosen the right event for my medal presentation. Perhaps it was fate and I knew in advance who was going to win the gold.

It seems to be the norm for sports stars to publish their biographies at the end of their careers. Chad le Clos, however, is not one to follow the norm and he has brought out his book at the beginning of his career. His achievements, which have been far from ordinary at this early stage, justify his story being told now.

And we look forward to even greater achievements from Chad in the future.

Sam Ramsamy
Member, IOC; vice president, International Swimming Federation; president, African Swimming Confederation; founding president, SSA

Dad on Chad – a few words from Bert le Clos

As I held up the South African flag and used it to wipe away my tears of joy, I found myself shouting out, 'Unbelievable!' I then remember saying, 'I have never been so happy in my life. It's like I have died and gone to heaven.'

I was simply overcome with the elation of seeing my son's name, Chad le Clos, appear as the gold medal winner for the 200 m butterfly at the London 2012 Olympic Games. His time: 1 minute 52.96 seconds.

As I was being interviewed by BBC sports presenter Clare Balding, I continued to watch the images of Chad, and I found myself again shouting, 'Unbelievable!'

I became synonymous with this word, and people associated it with me, but it really belonged to Chad – because of what he had achieved that memorable evening in London. I was just the messenger, whereas Chad was the message. It is only fitting that 'Unbelievable' should be the subtitle for Chad's biography.

The race was close all the way, but then, right at the finish, history was made for the Le Clos family. Could it be true that my son was now the winner of an Olympic gold medal? I looked at the results screen, which confirmed that he was: the gold was his. Mine was euphoria.

Before the race, people had been focusing on the world champion, Michael Phelps, and his quest to add to his phenomenal Olympic gold medal tally. Few had anticipated that Chad would have a chance, pitted against this great American swimmer. It was going to take something really special to upstage the champion. That 'something really special' came in the form of Chad le Clos that evening at the Olympic Park Aquatics Centre. He beat the person whom he admired and held in very high esteem. The narrow winning margin of 0.05 seconds didn't matter: as they say, an inch is as good as a mile.

My reaction was unprepared. It was the outflow of my emotions, brought on by the sheer excitement of witnessing the reward for my son's hard work and preparation over the years. I was a very proud father, and the tears were now streaming down my cheeks. I had not planned for this on television; I didn't know that I would be broadcast live all over the world. I didn't even have a handkerchief to wipe away the tears – hence the South African flag hanky. Many people say that image of me draped in the South African flag, sobbing like a baby, will forever be etched in their memories.

To add to my rapidly growing publicity, English recording artist and actress Lily Allen was sitting in front of me and tweeted about my response to her million-plus fans. But I honestly didn't care if the whole world was watching me cry. I believe that grown men should be able to express their emotions unrestrainedly.

TV presenter and former UK Olympic swimmer Mark Foster then located me and invited me for a quick interview. Security tried to stop me, but I was eventually cleared to go through to the media zone. I now found myself being interviewed on live television. It felt odd – I was just a fat guy who hadn't done anything great, unlike my son Chad. My claim to fame on the airwaves was to cry like a baby and wipe my tears with the South African flag.

As I sit back and try to analyse why I chose that word in that moment of Olympic glory for Chad, I find myself recalling the days when Chad was younger. I had travelled with him since he was little to his events, accompanying him around the country to numerous swim meetings. And now to see this culminate in an Olympic gold before my very eyes was, well, unbelievable.

'The father is more famous than the son,' people would say, tongue in cheek. I could not walk down the street without being stopped for a photo opportunity. Girls I didn't know would offer to buy me drinks if I stepped into a bar. Young mothers asked me to hold their babies so they could take photos. And, to top it all, I was nominated for the BBC Sports Personality of the Year Award, under the category of overseas sports personality. I am secretly relieved that the award eventually went to Jamaican sprinter Usain Bolt – a real athlete. The attention was all very flattering, but I wasn't the one who had won the gold medal. And as much as I joke about my newfound fame, it would not have been possible without Chad and his marvellous accomplishments. Though, I must admit, it has come about 30 years and 40 kilograms too late.

Through Chad's hard-earned efforts I have even appeared in my own TV advertisement – the one where, dressed in a tuxedo, I sing along to Nat King Cole's 'Unforgettable' (in my bad voice and all – I'm no Pavarotti, apart from a similar waistline, although I like to remind people that I used to look like Chad when I was younger), but instead, the words are changed to 'unbelievable'. I guess that makes me 'Nat King le Clos'. And it really is unbelievable – after all, I'm just a dad who is extremely proud of his son, just a fat oke from Durban! But the response to the ad was phenomenal. Even overseas, people would approach me and tell me they had seen the advert and liked it.

Of all the responses I have seen in the media to my reaction when Chad won gold, the one that he and I like the most is: 'Meet Bert le Clos. He just won the Olympic Games. He is London 2012.'

I would be lying if I said I didn't enjoy the attention. It has given me a glimpse of how fame and fortune may well cause people to lose their grounding, make them forget their ordinary beginnings. But I can confidently say this is not the case with my boy, Chad. His mother and I make it our duty to help him remain humble and true to his origins. Remarkably, despite his Olympic success, Chad has remained the same level-headed person he always was. We, his family, are the ones who see him every day, when the cameras are not rolling, and he has not allowed the rush of fame and money to change who he really is. This is what makes Chad so special and different.

I said in my BBC interview that evening, 'Look at him, he's beautiful.' When I said this, I was not referring to his physical good looks, but more to his inner beauty. It is my hope that through this book you will get a glimpse of this beauty.

It gives me great pleasure to be able to pen this preface for my son. Don't take my word for it, though. Read what others say about him and learn for yourself how special he is. You will also learn how he accomplished what can only be described as 'unbelievable'.

Bert le Clos

1 The journey begins

*'This is the last time you will ever get to race Michael
Phelps in the 200 m butterfly. If you want to beat him,
you have to beat him tonight.'*

These were my coach, Graham Hill's, last words to me before I went into
the call rooms to prepare myself for the start of the 200 m butterfly at the
London 2012 Games. Before I went in, I was hoping for some motivation
from Graham, and was expecting a lot more than this. Normally, Graham
would remind me about the plan for the race or go over technical details,
but not this time. I realised that was it.

But Graham's short message proved to be quite enough. That's why
Graham is the best and why we work so well together. He understands
me and knows exactly what to say to get me fired up. Graham's words
were effective in motivating me because what he said brought into clear
perspective all the previous years and kilometres of preparation that we
had both put in to get to where we were.

That evening, 31 July 2012, was destiny in the making. As Graham
and I later reflected, there was something special in the air. Even as we
made our way to the stadium, we just sensed something 'unbelievable'
was in the making.

And as you read, you will learn more of the role that Michael Phelps
played in inspiring me to do what I was doing. Watching the 2004 Athens
Olympics, I remember my dad calling for me to come and watch this swimming sensation, Michael Phelps, tearing it up in the pool. As a young kid,
I was so captivated by Michael's achievements that I recall telling my
family that I wanted to be like him. When I was little, I did what most
young boys did and used to imagine playing soccer alongside my heroes,
Ryan Giggs, Cristiano Ronaldo and Wayne Rooney. My dream of playing
for Manchester United immediately took a back seat – now I wanted
to become an Olympic champion, just like Michael Phelps. I hope this
decision didn't disappoint Sir Alex Ferguson! Anyway, Manchester United
has managed to do very well without me, I feel.

When Graham returned from the 2004 Olympics, I shared with him my desire to be a champion swimmer like Michael Phelps, and that is when I believe my journey to become an Olympic champion began.

In this book, I take you through how my dream became reality. I have my fair share of critics (mainly from the Phelps faithful) and people who say that it was just a touch of luck that won me the gold medal in 2012. I don't wish to make up your mind for you, but I encourage you to read on and judge for yourself whether I was lucky or not. And in the words of fellow South African Gary Player, 'the harder you practise, the luckier you become'.

I don't play down that winning touch: it has changed my life, and you probably wouldn't be reading this book or giving Chad le Clos a second thought had I not won.

I may still be young, but I have already learnt two invaluable lessons that have stood me in good stead thus far. Firstly, never give up your dreams and your goals. My family has taught me this. No matter who your competition is or who you are racing against, always finish confidently and believe in yourself.

There are many components that lead to success, but for me this was the biggest factor. I could have easily given up when I was swimming against the greatest Olympian swimmer ever. I was behind Phelps for most of the race and, were it not for this lesson, I may have been content to settle for the silver (still a formidable achievement). But Graham and I have always said we will fight to the end, and that's the code I live by.

The second lesson: don't get carried away with pride. Fame makes it a challenge to stay grounded. Some let success go to their heads and they become arrogant for various reasons – usually related to the financial rewards or power associated with success. I have vouched to be the same Chad le Clos I was before the gold.

I hope I have whetted your appetite to join me on this journey where you will meet the rest of my family. Many people already know my dad, but now meet all the other people who have helped me along this journey.

2 My first passion: soccer

'Get moving, you ballerina!'

That was my dad, in his unmistakable, deep voice, driving me on from the touchline during a soccer game. I was five. He was always at me because he felt that I was not playing hard enough or tackling with gusto. That's Dad for you – always approaching life with passion and enthusiasm. His positive attitude is infectious. He wears his heart on his sleeve, but never intends any harm. I recall that after that game, despite my poor performance (by his standards, anyway), he took me for ice cream. He has always had a big heart.

In his own days, my father was a good goalkeeper and played with the likes of the Bafana Bafana head coach, Gordon Igesund. I find it hard to imagine my dad as an agile goalkeeper, especially with the well-endowed physique he sports today (my tactful way to avoid saying that my father is a bit overweight).

My parents gave me the best chance possible to take part in whatever sport I chose. Soccer was the family sport, so it was natural that I happened to find myself on the soccer field. Soccer was my first love: I was around five when I first began playing football at Mandene Knights Football Club, Berea – although I didn't enjoy watching it much.

In the early days, my dad used to get frustrated with me, as, according to him, I wasn't a very good player. He claims I was more interested in eyeing the girls than focusing on the game, and he still teases me that my teammates' sisters used to tell him that they loved watching me play. He thinks it was because I never wanted to get my kit dirty. What can I say? I was under pressure – a hit with the ladies even back then.

Dad never pushed me into anything, but, nevertheless, he always wanted me to give my best and not muck around. I think it's sad when parents try to force sports on their children that they played in their own youth. My parents supported me, but never forced their own will on me. I've seen this with friends whose dads had played rugby and insisted their sons would do the same. This was never the case with my father. Had he chosen to relive his own youth through me, I would not have been a swimmer today, but a soccer player.

Who would have thought that the 'ballerina' would make the Kwa-Zulu-Natal soccer under-13s about five years later when I was 11? That's the thing I appreciate about my dad – he tells it like it is. Even today, it doesn't matter to him that I am an Olympic gold medallist. If he believes I can do something better or if I am wrong, he will pull me up. And I can rely on him to be honest. 'If you are not prepared for the truth, don't ask my dad,' we often joke.

I remember a particular match when my heart was just not in it. Afterwards Dad said, 'My boy, you are not a soccer player.' He wanted me to either take it seriously or choose another sport that might suit me better. He ensured that I attended soccer training twice a week and made the time for this despite his work commitments. Mum used to come along to video the matches and that's when I started acting up. On one occasion, I was more interested in posing for the camera than getting on with the game. This was the last straw for Dad – he gave me a 'red card' and marched me off the field.

Some may consider this a bit harsh, but it's this kind of tough love from my dad that ignited my ability to attempt anything with passion and de-termination, and never half-heartedly.

After that game, he was so disappointed that he told me he would not take me to the next training session. I remember crying. When I should have been at the next training appointment, Dad asked me to play soccer with him on the lawn instead. He showed me how to play with heart and taught me never to back down. As I mentioned earlier, Dad's enthusiasm is catching and his passion rubbed off on me. Later that week, he took me to the next training session and afterwards I recall the coach asking my father what had happened to me and whether he had been feeding me raw meat. He had observed a huge difference in my game since the previous session. This was largely due to my attitude, which was now more positive; I showed greater urgency and drive. I played in defence and had made sure that no one got past me in that training session. It was all thanks to my father, who had made it clear to me that, whatever I did, I had to give my best. My dad's reply to the coach? 'I did what I had to do to make sure my son doesn't play like a ballerina!'

I think this intervention was crucial: it ignited my desire to play sport with passion. This was when my 'winning attitude', as my coach Graham Hill later put it, started to bloom.

I had gained a reputation as a hard player and a tough tackler at Mandene Knights, so I was made captain. Not bad – from ballerina to captain of the team. My position was 'last man', or centre back, and my job was to make sure that no opposition player got past me.

Some would say that I verged on being a dirty player. I prefer to think I was just a tough tackler. In my position as 'last man', or centre back, this style of play was necessary to make sure that the opposition for-wards did not have it easy trying to get past me. But in one game we played, there was a taller, older guy who managed to get through. I was so enraged that I remember chasing after him and rugby-tackling him from behind, grabbing him around his waist. I quickly got to my feet and apologised to him and to the referee. I claimed that I had slipped and accidentally fallen on him. Thank God there was no video referee in those days, otherwise I would have certainly got a red card and perhaps even been banned for several matches.

At that club, I was the big fish, but when I turned 11, I switched to a club in Umbilo, Durban. I suddenly found myself among some really good players and the coach changed my position from centre back to left back, so I could be involved in the attack. Playing among the better players meant my game improved, and I remember making the Pinetown and Districts Football Association under-12 side.

Thanks to my father's influence, I had learnt to give my all in soccer and I soon gained a reputation. Some opposition players would hear me charging after them and would put the ball into touch to avoid an en-counter. Before one particularly important game, our coach told us that there was a dangerous attacking player, a certain Robbie, in the opposition, who was fast and talented, and who was going to pose a big threat to us. One of our players asked what we were going to do about him, to which the coach replied, 'Simple, we put our killer on him, the full stop – Chad le Clos!' My instructions were clear: stick on Robbie and do what I had to do so he couldn't get past me.

I recall Robbie haring down the wing; he pushed the ball past me. There was no way I was going to catch him, as he was much faster than me, so as he tried to come around me I tripped him. It was a foul, but as Robbie got up he retaliated by kicking out at me. That resulted in both of us being sent off. Mission accomplished, though, as I had neutralised our biggest threat. The good news is that we went on to win 3-1. My dad says that I was so fanatical about doing what the coach wanted and so driven that I used to run non-stop during matches and once collapsed from sheer exhaustion.

My soccer talents got me into the KwaZulu-Natal team as a defender in Grade 7. I had to stop playing provincial football, however, when I was around 13 due to my swimming commitments. Since Grade 5, I had been attending swimming practice after school in Pinetown from 3 to 4:30 p.m. and then had to rush back for soccer practice at 5 p.m. This was my routine on Mondays, Wednesdays and Fridays – then I played football on Saturday too.

As I continued playing soccer, I moved out of defence into midfield and eventually played as a striker. I was a Manchester United fan and liked Cristiano Ronaldo's attacking style of play. I used to practise his moves in our yard in Pinetown with my brother Jordan. Every day after swimming training, I would come home and Jordan and I would kick the ball about. This was our Old Trafford, and I recall scoring many goals for Manchester United there. After swim training, my swimming buddies and I used to play Reds versus Blues in a seven- or eight-a-side game once a month – the Manchester United versus Chelsea Challenge, as we called it.

We loved soccer so much that the rain would not stop us. We would even put on our swimsuits and play in the rain.

I also played rugby – on the wing, because of my speed – but I dropped it, as I was not one for tackling. When I reached 16, I was not as quick as the others because my feet became flatter, which, although not good for running, was an advantage for swimming.

It was hard for me to give up soccer, but I had to make a tough decision when, at 15, I sustained a severe groin injury which seriously affected my ability to swim a proper breaststroke.

So, at the age of 16, for the future of my swimming career, I made the decision to stop kicking a ball.

Young talent: from swimming teacher to swimming coach

'Chad, it would be better if you did not swim the butterfly. You are not swimming it correctly.'

My father's family hails from the beautiful Indian Ocean island of Mauritius, which is perhaps why people say I resemble a fish in water. My father emigrated to South Africa when he was nine. At that time, he couldn't speak a word of English, as he is from a French-speaking family. On my mother's side, there is Afrikaner heritage, so, overall, I consider myself proudly South African.

Dad says that he fancied my mum the first time he saw her at Club Med, a popular nightclub in Durban at the time. He asked her out for drinks but she played hard to get and told him that she didn't go out with drunkards. Dad took offence but was nevertheless not prepared to back down. Sometime later, Mum's friend Sandy asked Dad for a dance. Sandy pointed to Mum and said, 'See that girl there with the beautiful smile and great looks. She absolutely adores you.' The rest is history.

They were married on 18 August 1990 at the Methodist church in Glenwood, Durban. They had a little flat on the Durban beachfront and Dad had just started a butchery business, Bert's Meat Market. It seems they were a glamorous couple before I came along and my mother was the belle of the ball. I was born at Westville Hospital on 12 April 1992. My paternal grandmother made it a point to be at the birth of every one of her grandchildren.

My parents enrolled me at a day-care centre, where I was introduced to swimming from a very tender age. Dad also took me into our pool at home, despite my mother's protests. Being very young, I was initially terrified and would cry hysterically, I'm told. And I was not the only one in tears. Mum also cried and said to Dad, 'My baby, my baby, bring me back my baby,' as he took me further into the pool.

I can assure you that I don't cry when I am in the pool any more. Well, except perhaps for that time at the 2012 London Olympics, when I realised I had beaten Michael Phelps and won the gold. Other than that, the tears are no more and I can safely say that I have come to rather enjoy my time in the pool.

I began primary school in 1998, a year earlier than was required (goes to show how keen my parents were to get rid of me, I guess!). It was the same year that my younger brother, Jordan, was born. It was at Penzance Primary School, near my parents' home in Glenwood, that I began to take swimming seriously.

By the time I had reached Grade 4, the one-year age disadvantage between me and my classmates was beginning to have a marked effect on my ability to compete in sports. My parents, therefore, chose to hold me back a year so that I would be among kids of the same age. The plan didn't go down well and I copped a lot of flak at school – I was teased that

I had remained behind because I had failed Grade 4. I was not happy to remain in Grade 4. I was a shy child with not many friends, and it knocked my confidence. But one benefit of repeating Grade 4 was that I got an 'A' aggregate for the year (unsurprisingly, as I had already done the school-work the previous year), but, yes, I can still boast that I was an 'A' student. From a confidence perspective, repeating the grade was also beneficial for my swimming.

My primary school was a turning point. At Penzance, my school swim-ming teacher was Ms Manthey, who played a big role in my early swimming development. Our club was called the Penzance Pirates. Initially, swimming didn't mean as much to me as soccer, tennis or rugby. But even though I didn't dedicate myself to swimming at that stage, after six months of coaching me, Lindsay Manthey recommended to my parents that I under-took professional coaching, as she could see I had talent.

Lindsay was a graduate from Edgewood Teachers' College where she had specialised in physical education. In 1985 she became the swimming coach at Penzance Primary. Since the age of 12, she had always been involved in swimming and had represented KwaZulu-Natal high schools. At Penzance she started giving extra swimming lessons in her private capacity. When she spotted a child's talent, she referred them to other coaches who were able to fine-tune their skills, and where they would have the opportunity to swim all year round, as Penzance didn't have a heated pool for the winter months. This way, Lindsay provided a very efficient nursery for the kids at Penzance who were keen on swimming, and she was highly regarded by other coaches for her development of young swimming talent.

Says Lindsay:

One of the youngsters was way above anyone else I had ever coached. At the time he joined my swimming classes, Chad was eight or nine years old and in Grade 3. I knew there was something different about him. After the first few months, I said to his parents, 'Your boy is really good.'

What separated Chad from the rest of the kids was his incredible determination and work ethic, even at that age. It was very unusual to see this in such a young child. He was also much faster than some of the older boys. At the end of the season, I spoke to his parents again and said that he had so much talent that he really needed to be with a more professional coach where he could swim through the winter. I was cautious in my recommendation, though, as over the years, I had seen many kids burn out. This was largely because they did not get coaching appropriate to their age, and I certainly didn't want that for Chad.

It was Lindsay who suggested to my parents that they contact Graham Hill, a professional swimming coach she recommended. I can't begin to say how much I owe her for this. Lindsay explains how she first put me and my coach in contact:

> Swimming is unlike other sports. People who don't swim don't realise the effect of sensory deprivation. You are completely alone when you swim, as your key sense organs, your ears and eyes, are submerged in the water. I have watched kids with incredible talent lose the mental capacity to carry on to further greatness because of the strenuous demands of swimming. So I assured Bert and Geraldine that I was going to do my best to help find the right coach for Chad so that we could be sure he would still be swimming in his 20s, and have the mental strength required for greatness.
>
> I could see that Chad had a mental drive that set him apart, but I was not going to chance him to a naive coach. After I had researched the professional swimming coaches around at the time, Graham Hill stood out. I had not met or spoken to Graham, but from feedback I knew that he was among the best. He had been a Springbok swimmer and would therefore understand the demands of the sport, mentally and physically. I was confident that he would nurture Chad's incredible talent and wouldn't let him burn out.

So to what extent had Ms Manthey been able to glimpse my talent? Had I shown signs of potential greatness back in junior school?

> Having someone like him in our school swimming team was great. At primary school level, all swimming is done in a team and you therefore need all four team members to perform well. I recall, at times, that before our team would be heading into the final leg, we would be lagging fifth or sixth. Then Chad would dive in and he would see to it that we finished first.

But I had no idea that, at that young age, he would go on to be an Olympic swimmer. I would never put that expectation or immense pressure on any child. I believe that it is dangerous for coaches to place such pressure on young kids. But I do recall that in Grade 6, Chad had started to say that he was going to swim at the Olympics one day. This came from him, though – no one else.

In what ways does Lindsay feel that the Olympic gold might have changed me, her young junior-school protégé?

I was Chad's class teacher for English and social sciences. I recall that his manners were impeccable and that he had excellent values. After Chad won the world championships, he would come to school to fetch his younger brother, Jordan, and he would stop and greet his ex-teachers. He always had time to say a kind word even after he had become a world champ. When the press visited Penzance Primary, they interviewed Ellen Khanyile, the tea lady. It turns out that Chad used to offer to help carry her trays and do the washing up. I admire this quality in Chad. He has more than just an Olympic gold: he has a heart of gold. And despite his fame, he remains a positive role model.

I watched Chad win that 200 m butterfly Olympic final from home, but I think they must have heard my screams in London. It was the most thrilling moment in sport that I have ever experienced, and I watch a lot of sport. I guess the personal connection I had with Chad and the Le Clos family made it even more special. In Chad's momentous victory, I saw the beginning and the end, and knowing I had played a small part in this incredible story was more than enough for me. Now, as I near retirement, I would never have given up being a teacher for that one moment when Chad won an Olympic gold. It made it all worth it.

Thanks to Lindsay, Graham Hill has been my coach since 2000, when I was eight years old. I would also like to thank Penzance Primary School for the support they gave me during the 2012 Olympics. When I had qualified for the Olympics, they erected a big board at the school with the words 'Penzance Primary supports Chad le Clos' Olympic dream'. And when I made the final, the school put up banners saying 'Good luck, Chad'. I guess that's how the press knew of the school's connection with me.

From the outset, I want to say how grateful I am to my parents for making the sacrifices they did so that I can be the success I am today. At the time, we were living in Glenwood and Graham was giving coaching in Pinetown – quite a distance to travel four times a week. That's why I'm grateful to them for ensuring that I got to the coaching sessions, despite the inconvenience. Dad didn't mind. He said he wanted me to be trained by the best, so the travelling was not a problem. And when my swimming started to get serious when I was about 13, I began training in the mornings as well. Mum had to wake up at 4:30 a.m. to take me to coaching before going to work. Dad would do the afternoon shifts.

Initially, I trained at Graham's house. In those days, I was not that fast. My parents could not understand this and asked why I was always at the back of the pool. My dad even became frustrated, so I explained to him that my friend, Ntotuko, was quite slow and I didn't want him to feel lonely at the back. Dad was sympathetic, but pointed out that I wasn't really helping Ntotuko and that I should swim my fastest.

In another incident that I can recall at one of our coaching sessions, a boy who was a national champ and a bit older than me said, 'Chad, it would be better if you did not swim the butterfly. You are not swimming it correctly, so I think it's best that you give up butterfly.'

I looked up to this guy, as he was my senior and he used to lap me consistently at training. He would go for eight laps and I would still be trailing in the sixth. I think he had good intentions in telling me this. However, I am glad that I did not listen to him. Who would have thought that, some ten years later, I would become Olympic champ at the 200 m butterfly?

My swimming was improving with Graham's coaching, and I was selected to represent my province, KwaZulu-Natal, in my age group. So this meant that we used to travel around the country for the inter-provincial swim meets. My first national gala was in 2002; it was held in the Cape. I only managed a bronze in the 200 m breaststroke that year. But my parents and coach encouraged me that it was a good start.

For the gala we stayed with my Aunt Dominique, my dad's sister. Her house had a pool which I used to love playing in with my cousin, Guy Francis. One day, eager to get in, I ended up cracking my front tooth in half when I dove head first into the shallow end after miscalculating just how deep it was. I couldn't find the part of my tooth that I lost, but immediately went to the dentist, who capped my tooth.

The next day, on Saturday, Guy and I were playing 'stingers' in the pool – a game that involves dodging a ball being thrown at you at the risk of being 'stung' by it. At one point, after I ducked to avoid the ball Guy was throwing at me, I hit my tooth against the pool wall. The capping on my tooth came off and, although I was afraid to do so, I had to show my dad what had happened to me because it was really painful and he would have found out eventually.

We went to a popular amusement park in Cape Town the next day. This wasn't a very pleasant experience as the capping on my tooth hadn't been fixed because there wasn't a dentist available over the weekend – so it hurt every time I opened my mouth. The pain meant I couldn't enjoy the ride on the park's 'Cobra One', one of the fastest rides around, and the one I was really looking forward to. I was quick to visit the dentist on Monday after that. But was the fact that I chipped my tooth twice in a pool a sign of future luck to come?

3 The birth of my dream

'You see, I was right, they must be doctoring his results!'

With my emerging success in swimming, people started taking notice of me. When I was 12, I was selected for the KwaZulu-Natal Lifesavers, part of Lifesaving South Africa, a registered member of the South African Sports Confederation and Olympic Committee. The organisation mainly exists to provide a voluntary lifeguard service that benefits our communities at large. The irony is that I had never had any previous experience in surf lifesaving. I was selected purely on the basis of my reputation as a swimmer. Swimming in the sea, however, is rather different from swimming in a pool. To this day, the only waves I really enjoy are the ones I make with my swimming accolades in the pool.

The National Lifesaving Champs were held at Cape Town's Strand beach that year, an event I remember for the wrong reasons. I recall nearly getting decapitated. I was late for my race and had to run from one end of the beach to the other. The next thing, my dad says, my feet were in the air. I had collided full speed with a rope, which caught me in the neck. I was badly winded and people around me thought I was dead as I lay motionless on the sand. My neck got badly scarred – a relic of my surf lifesaving days.

I didn't fair too well in the swimming leg during that competition. Like I said, I don't like surf swimming. We all dived into the water and were confronted by the immense False Bay waves that I had to swim against. I was not enjoying it, and after a while I stuck my hand up – the signal to get the attention of the organisation officials on the nearby boat. Dad remembers what a sorry sight I was when they pulled me out of the water.

My first attempts at surfing were certainly a better experience than swimming in the sea, although Dad still gets hysterical when he remembers how intimidated I was by the big waves. I remember going down to the beach with my dad. He was standing with one of the surfing officials, and says I amazed everyone because it was my first time surfing and I was able to stand up on the board. One of the officials turned to my dad and said, 'Bert, you are lying – this can't be Chad's first time. He must have been practising.'

Because of the early promise I showed, Dad got me a customised board made by board-maker Peter Daniels. But, like my lifesaving episode, my surfing days also proved to be short-lived. I recall the surf was rough, which made me hesitant to take on any waves. This was testing my dad's patience and he shouted out, 'Take the wave, you ballerina!' My response to him was, 'No. You take the wave!' I was too afraid to venture in.

All credit to him, though, as, when he realised that I was not enjoying surfing, he did the common-sense thing and let me quit. Today it is a different story. I love surfing and look forward to getting away from the pressure and catching the waves near Durban's North Beach. When I am surfing I feel relaxed – I find it's an excellent de-stressor.

My best de-stressor has always been my dad. He has such a good sense of humour. Once, when I was around nine, we went for a family vacation to Mauritius. Dad had arranged for his cousin to watch the house and feed our dog and goldfish. When Dad's cousin had fetched us from the airport he was gutted, as the goldfish had died. He was really remorseful and blamed himself for the death. Dad being Dad and seeing the opportunity, asked his cousin, 'But did you feed the rabbit?'

This set him into panic mode and he was extremely worried and apologised even more profusely, 'Sorry, Bert I didn't feed the rabbit, because I couldn't find the rabbit. Maybe I let him escape unintentionally when I opened the gate.' I came to the rescue, saying to my dad with my lisp, 'But, Dadth, we don't haveth a rabbithh.'

I had been an animal lover from when I was little. When the boys my age had cars and action figurines, I was into little plastic animal toys. Growing up, I think I must have had hundreds of them. When my family threw the milk cartons into the bin, I would remove them and cut out the pictures of the cows because I didn't want them landing up in the bin. When people visited, I would want to know if they liked animals and would ask, 'Are you a cow person or a people person?'

Panic in the pool

When I was in Grade 6, we travelled to Germiston for a national swim meet. Before that event, I had not lost in the 200 m breaststroke for the past three years in my age group, so I was the favourite to win this race.

I don't know exactly what happened. It was very cold in the East Rand compared to the climate I was accustomed to in Durban. As I dived into the pool, I was startled by the icy-cold water. At the 100 m mark – I don't know whether it was my asthma (I had been diagnosed with it when I was seven) that acted up or a panic attack – I stopped at the wall. I felt embarrassed, as I had been the favourite to win. After a few seconds, I managed to regain my composure and started to chase the others. Even though I was way behind the field, I still managed to finish a respectable third. I was extremely disappointed, as I could have won the gold had I not freaked out. As I got out of the pool, I could hear people saying, 'Did you see how Chad came back in the last 50 m after he stopped? It was incredible!'

That incident of panic brought it home to me that swimming can be a very lonely sport. The public doesn't understand how mentally tough it can be. Ask any swimmer, and they will tell you how challenging it is when they are isolated in the pool looking at the black line at the bottom.

Someone who witnessed that incident in Germiston was Delon Dannhauser, the assistant coach at Seagulls, my swimming club in Durban. He was based in Gauteng at the time and his son, Wade, and I were provincial rivals competing in the same age group. In 2004 Wade and I competed at the Interprovincial Primary School Championship in Bloemfontein in the under-12 age group, the first time we had raced against each other. Later, when Delon first came to Seagulls to coach, he admitted that he was sceptical about my times and even suspected that they were doctored.

Delon remembers that Germiston race:

This was the first time I had seen Chad swim. He had some sort of asthma or panic attack. I turned to my wife and said, 'You see, I was right, they must be doctoring his results!' However, when I saw Chad catch up, I realised he possessed some extraordinary quality. He was way behind the rest of the field and yet he managed to finish third.

'In the 12–14 age group, no other swimmer had a chance against Chad,' says Delon. 'He would win the 200 m breaststroke every time. In all my coaching years, I had never seen anyone swim such a good 200 m breaststroke.'

Two weeks after the Germiston episode, Delon met me again at another competition, this time in Pietermaritzburg. 'Here Chad showed his class again when he improved on his times and won the 200 m breaststroke,' says Delon. 'I think that, apart from that panic episode, Chad never lost an age-group race in the 200 m breaststroke. He has picked up from where South African swimmer Terence Parkin left off under Graham Hill.'

In 2007 Delon moved to Durban, where he coached at the Pisces Swimming Club. He set up a high-performance centre, which entailed a more scientific approach to coaching, including video analysis, a flume pool (which generates a current) and the use of a mirror at the bottom of the pool so that swimmers can analyse their technique.

In swimming circles in South Africa, it is widely known that Graham Hill produces consistently some of the best swimmers and, as a coach, he is rated very highly by his peers. Says Delon: 'When I had a chance to work with Graham, I grabbed it with both hands. He advised me to go to Australia's Gold Coast to complete a silver-licence course.'

While Delon was in Australia, his wife had to go to Seagulls to meet Graham. Because of all the years of inter-club rivalry, she was anxious. 'We had formed the impression that these Seagulls people were arrogant, but Chad walked over to her and said, "Welcome to Seagulls – so glad to have you." We were very pleasantly surprised by the courtesy we were extended at Seagulls.'

Delon continues:

When I joined Seagulls in 2010, I was asked to take times for Chad, and my mouth would be left hanging open. I now take it all back when I say I had suspected his times were doctored. Chad is a remarkable athlete and, mentally, has the ability to go where few people can. I watch in admiration as he trains. Taking his times is a privilege. He has a unique ability not to give up. He doesn't like anyone beating him – even at training. His self-belief is extraordinary, but he doesn't overshoot himself, as he knows himself very well. I have observed that no one can train like him, and we have some very good swimmers at the club.

I recall watching the Olympics 200 m butterfly final with his whole family at the Stella Football Club, and I remember what Chad had said to us three months before: "I will win the 200 m butterfly." Such was his self-belief. The final was the realisation of a dream almost ten years in the making. It was a privilege and honour for me to have been part of this – just for the last two years – and the highlight of my career.

What does Delon think of my future prospects? 'The world has not seen the best of him yet,' he says. 'He has the ability to dominate the sport for the next ten years. He has the support to achieve it with a coach like Graham Hill and parents like Bert and Geraldine. Having known Chad before London 2012, I can say that he hasn't let the fame go to his head – the trait of a true champion!'

I went to Westville Boys High School (WBHS) in 2006. It's a prestigious school with a long history going back to the 1860s, when German immigrant farmers first opened a school in the area. In 1999, WBHS was rated the best state-aided school in South Africa in a survey conducted by the *Sunday Times*. Following the 2006 matric results, WBHS joined an elite group of only 13 schools in the country that achieved more than 100 passes in maths at the higher grade – the only school in Kwa-Zulu Natal have this accolade. One of my teachers, Mr Bull, had also taught my father. I carried on the tradition in another sense, as my coach, Graham, is also a WBHS alumnus.

As the school swimming captain, I dreaded having to give speeches after our weekend galas during school assembly. I could never handle public speaking, and had to resort to lots of 'umms' and 'ahs'. In fact, I didn't enjoy Grade 7 much, as swimming was not as popular as rugby, cricket or hockey. I also recall that the year-end dance for Grade 7 was a shocker for me. It was a 'Survivor' theme, and I refused to dance because I was so worried about what the others would think of me. I was afraid to make a fool of myself.

I was disappointed not to have been selected to be a prefect, but I did get the Sports Boy of the Year award in 2005. That to me felt like a well-deserved tribute for all young swimmers, who were overshadowed by the rugby, cricket and soccer players.

In 2004, my family had moved house to Westville. This was around the time of the Athens Olympics and the first time I became aware of Michael Phelps. I particularly remember him swimming in the 400 m individual medley (IM), which has been staged as the first event in the Olympics swimming programme since 1912.

I was awestruck by Phelps. He qualified first with a time of 4:08.8.

He destroyed that Olympic field, which had some pretty strong swimmers. I recall saying to myself that this is what I wanted to do and who I wanted to be like. Phelps was going for eight gold medals. In the end, he got six golds and two bronzes. And it was the South African relay team that denied him by winning the gold in the 4 x 100 m relay – a team that included Ryk, Roland, Linden and Darian. South Africa basically stopped Phelps from getting his eight golds. If he had, he would have beaten Mark Spitz's record haul of seven gold medals in the 1972 Munich Olympics.

Having seen him perform in the 2004 Olympics, I started admiring Phelps. That was when my own desire to become an Olympic champion took root.

Michael Fred Phelps II was born on 30 June 1985. The youngest of three children, Phelps began swimming at the age of seven, partly because of the influence of his sisters and partly to provide him with an outlet for his energy, as he had been diagnosed with attention deficit hyperactivity disorder (ADHD). By the age of ten, he held a national record for his age group, and began to train at the North Baltimore Aquatic Club under coach Bob Bowman.

Phelps's rapid improvement culminated in him qualifying for the 2000 Summer Olympics at the age of 15 and becoming the youngest male to make a US Olympic swim team in 68 years.

Phelps is the most decorated Olympian of all time, with a total of 22 medals. He also holds the all-time record for Olympic gold medals (at 18 golds). By winning eight gold medals at the 2008 Beijing Games, Phelps took the record for the most first-place finishes at any single Olympic Games. In the 2012 Summer Olympics in London, Phelps won four gold and two silver medals, making him the most successful athlete of the Games for the third Olympics in a row.

Phelps's international titles and record-breaking performances have earned him the World Swimmer of the Year Award seven times, as well as the International Swimming Federation (FINA) Swimmer of the Year Award in 2012.

Graham Hill was the South African team coach, and when he returned from the Athens Olympics I shared with Graham my dream to be like Michael Phelps. Graham understood this and that is when our preparation began for the realisation of my Olympic dream. From my experiences thus far, I know that anything worthwhile in life starts with a desire, a dream. This sentiment was summarised by the headline in a local newspaper,

'Young Chad le Clos says he will go to 2012 Olympics'. Watching Michael Phelps at the 2004 Athens Olympics was my inspiration.

In 2005 a businessman who wishes to remain anonymous, and who had read an article about my accolades in swimming, sponsored a trip to the UK for an event where some of the best juniors in the world were competing. It was an invitational meeting where foreigners could pit their skills against the best swimmers in the UK in their age group. Graham thought it would be useful for me to go so he could get a better idea of where I was in comparison to some of the best in the world. There were three other South Africans at that competition: Michael Meyer, Heinrich Alberts and Natasha Warren Stone. I was fortunate to have had my expenses financed. With the competition being so tough, in the end I only managed to qualify for three races. For the 200m breaststroke, I managed 2.42 and made the final in lane 8. I thought the other guys were going to tire, but I ended up finishing last out of eight. I also finished eighth in the 100 m breaststroke and the 400 m IM.

We did not achieve the results we wanted for South Africa, having gone into the tournament thinking we would do well. Only Heinrich achieved anything of significance by getting a silver. I felt really bad, as I had nothing to show my sponsor for his support.

However, I didn't allow this disappointment to take my eyes off my dream, or my focus away from wanting to be an Olympic champ. I feel that you start to see obstacles when you take your eyes off your goal.

The best way to describe Graham Hill is as someone who is also very passionate about swimming. Having been a South African national swimmer, he understands the pressures that swimmers experience, and he always pushes me to go all the way. There is no such thing as half measures with Graham – it's all or nothing, and that's one of the reasons he is such a great coach.

Graham has been coaching swimming since 1985. His mother, Doreen, founded the Seagulls club in 1987 after having been the head coach at Westville Swimming Club in the 1970s and early 1980s. Graham started his coaching career under her supervision when she allocated ten swimmers to his charge. In his early coaching days, his mother was his mentor and when she retired, Graham became the head coach at Seagulls. In February 2011, Graham was appointed head coach for Swimming South Africa.

Graham recalls his first impressions of me when we met in 2000:

When his parents brought Chad to my swimming club, Seagulls, his father mentioned that his schoolteacher had recommended that they bring him to me, as she had said he had talent. Parents often tell me how talented their children are. I prefer to get them into the water to see how they really perform. I make no assumptions and give them all an equal chance.

But in Chad's case, I did observe early on that he possessed something special, which was evident from that early age. And he was always very eager to train and do everything that I required of him. Because of my commitments with senior swimmers, there were times when I had to be away from the club. This was when Chad's dedication to training came to the fore. His uncle had come to fetch him one day from his training session and was waiting for him. He noticed that the other kids were already leaving the club, so, thinking that the session was over, he asked where Chad was. They told him that Chad was still swimming. About 20 minutes later, when Chad finally arrived, his uncle asked him why he was still swimming when the others had already left. Chad told him that his coach had asked them to swim 3.5 kilometres, but because he (the coach) was not there, they had decided to leave early. This story illustrates Chad's attitude from a young age and his dedication to training. It doesn't surprise me that Chad has gone on to achieve the great results he has. Upcoming youngsters should learn from Chad's positive attitude and remember that, to become a champion, it all starts with how well you train. Success requires dedication to training.

Since he first saw my potential, Graham has always worked with me to bring it out. He wanted me to be the best in the world, and not just in Kwa-Zulu Natal or South Africa. He is big on discipline and that's a reason why he gets the results. He is very driven and has a hunger for success, which is why I see him in the mould of figures like Sir Alex Ferguson. Importantly, Graham and I understand each other well, and at times we even know what the other is thinking. I respect Graham a lot and have learnt a great deal from him. He employs tactical thinking with all our races and is very meticulous. He is also a great friend. Graham says:

As Chad has recounted, when he was around 12 or 13 he swam at a British age-group meeting. He was disappointed that he didn't win anything, and I could see that he was determined to win. That is something I believe you can't teach, that winning attitude. I could see that he had this special attitude. He had that X-factor, or the killer instinct to win, a desire to succeed at the highest level. For a coach, it's important that your students naturally possess this attitude: it is not something that can be coached.

Chad's approach towards training after that disappointment in the UK was significantly different. He became even more determined to improve. He knew where he needed to be in terms of his times and he set about improving them, starting with training.

As the training became increasingly intense, I had to juggle my school work with swimming commitments. Dave Rankin has been a friend since my early days at Seagulls. 'I can remember Chad bringing his school work to training, as he was away most of the time from school,' says Dave. 'At training I can remember him getting help from some of the older guys – which showed how much he was keen to excel at school as well.'

Dave also remembers a less well-known, less serious side:

Chad always trained hard and was very focused, as his coaches have said. But he did well to hide from them his other side – the prankster side. I remember once at training he had us in stitches of laughter. He had drawn under his clothes, on his bare skin, a swimming suit – even with the Arena logo on it and all the details – with a marker pen. Then, in full view of the others, he proceeds to take off all of his clothes down to his 'swimming trunks'.

I have seen how Chad's determination and hunger for success have made him who he is today. But, as his friend, I would like people to know that what I admire in him is that he hasn't let the fame and attention get to his head. He still has time for people and keeps in touch with his friends. He is an extremely talented athlete and a dear friend.

Rene Warnes, another member of Seagulls, has been training with me for over six years:

> We enjoy training with Chad, as he keeps it light-hearted and enjoyable. People would expect an Olympic gold medallist to be serious, but Chad strikes a good balance. He keeps all of us motivated, especially the younger ones, whom you often hear Chad encouraging: 'Carry on, don't give up.'
>
> He inspires us and wants us all to do our best. He also takes time to watch others compete. I wouldn't expect that from a world-famous champ, who you would expect to be engrossed in his own world – but not Chad le Clos.

A school friend, Jayden Fourie, can recall the pranks we got up to at Westville Boys High despite the heavily disciplined atmosphere of its hallowed corridors. I already knew Jayden from swimming galas, and from his very first day at Westville Boys, I suspect he knew I was going to make his life a misery. Jayden recalls a few experiences:

> Before some provincial swimming race, Chad was standing there with his hood on, posturing like a boxer before a fight, trying to intimidate me. But I won that race – it was the 50 m butterfly. I remember his father was peeved. Perhaps that's why I had it coming to me. On my very first day at Westville Boys, I had a feeling there was going to be trouble. Chad charmingly offered to show the new boy the ropes. At the time, I thought that was a pleasant gesture. The first thing he did, though, was send me to a strictly out-of-bounds part of the school, where I was immediately shocked to find myself muscled out by a gang of senior prefects and sent packing with a stern warning, barely escaping detention on day one.
>
> On another occasion, on a final warning, standing in the heavily bearded disciplinarian teacher's office, I have my head bowed in chastisement, attempting hopelessly to be serious and respectful. I'm facing expulsion, and it could go badly wrong. Suddenly, Chad appears in the window, gesturing at the master's beard, and I burst out laughing. Chad clearly had in mind the school motto, *Incepto Ne Desistam* ('May I not shrink from my purpose'), because the pranks never stopped. There was 'that occasion in matric with the Pritt stick'

that Chad threw at the teacher when her back was turned. Daring, perhaps – only, the Pritt stick mysteriously had my name on it ... Some of you may be asking why I am still his friend after all these years of abuse. Chad has a great sense of balance, which makes him such a good friend. He is deeply serious about his ambitions to be the best in his sport, but at the same time he can certainly be a barrel of laughs.

Another close friend of mine from school days is Leith 'Shanky' Shankland. We also swim together for Seagulls. Our friendship was established during our high-school days. He is blessed with great talent as a swimmer and is very intelligent. Shanky helped and guided me a lot for my final exams in my matric year. He was also my fellow team member and roommate for the 2012 Olympics.

'It's good to know that I was part of Chad's support crew for his final exams,' says Shanky. 'He got three As in matric – history, life orientation and maths. This is a great achievement when you consider that Chad was away from school for more than half that year. He is a bright person and has a very good memory.'

Leaving my pranks aside, let me talk to you about a brief history of swimming in South Africa.

The history of swimming in South Africa goes back to 1899, when the first national swimming association was established: the South African Amateur Swimming Union (SAASU). It was present in two provinces at the time, Eastern Province and Western Province. In 1908, FINA was founded and by 1909 SAASU was accepted as a member of FINA.

The first time a South African swimmer took part in the Olympic Games was at the 1912 Games, and in 1928 South Africa won its first swimming medal at the Olympic Games in Amsterdam. South African swimmers represented their country at the 1934 Empire Games in London, the 1938 Empire Games in Sydney and the 1948 Olympic Games in London.

Due to international sports boycotts as a result of apartheid, South Africa was expelled from FINA in 1973, but in 1992 the country was re-admitted and allowed to compete at the Barcelona Olympics. Swimming South Africa, the umbrella body governing swimming in South Africa, was established in 1994. SSA's main objective is to develop, control and promote all aquatic disciplines in South Africa. In 1995, South Africa took part in the All-Africa Games for the first time.

In the international arena, the US and Australia have dominated professional swimming for a long time and European countries have always been a major force. The emerging nations today are China, Japan and Brazil.

The biggest challenge facing swimmers who want to become professional in South Africa is finances. The sport doesn't attract big sponsors, as do other, more popular sports like rugby, soccer and cricket. This is a situation that I am hoping to change for the better.

4 Entering the international arena

'If the best in the world was doing a 1 000 m cool down, then I was certainly not going to do anything less.'

In 2006, I made the Kwa-Zulu Natal high school team and at the end of the year was selected for the squad to compete in Perth for the Western Australia Championship. It was a breakthrough year for me: I very much wanted to improve my competition performance after my disappointing results at the UK event the previous year. All the hard work that I had put in after returning from England paid off, as I came back with three gold medals, three silvers and three bronzes. I also broke the South African junior record for the under-14 age group.

The Australian event was the starting point for my improved international performances. And the following year, 2007, I was back to Australia. In Grade 9 (at the age of 15), I went on a school sports tour to Sydney, Brisbane and the Gold Coast, where we were pitted against the best swimmers in Australia in our age group. Westville Boys High performed very well and since then has been among the top-performing swimming schools in South Africa.

The Rugby World Cup was held that year and the whole squad stayed up till 4 a.m. to watch the Springboks hammer England in the pool game. Little did I realise at the time that, four years later, I would get to meet one of the stars of that World Cup and one of our country's greatest Springboks, Victor Matfield, at the Minister of Sport's Indaba.

We had a very strong team for that Australia tour and won the overall log. The emphasis was on school relays, as opposed to individual races, because the whole purpose of the tour was for us to gain competition experience. It was tough, as the Aussies are renowned for their competitiveness, but it was also a fun tour. One of the highlights for me was getting the chance to surf at Sydney's Bondi Beach.

In 2007, I also had to make the decision to stop playing soccer and tennis completely, as I realised I had to focus solely on my swimming, and I also had a groin-strain issue. The following year would see the trials for the 2008 Beijing Olympics, the 2009 World Cup and the 2010 Commonwealth Games, to be held in India. I was now in the senior high-school team, with breaststroke being my main stroke as well as the IM.

I made the finals at the South African Nationals in 2008, held in Kings Park, Durban, but came fourth in the 400 m IM, finishing out of the medal placing that year. Graham went with the South African swimming team to the 2008 Beijing Olympics. I followed the Games on TV. I was supporting Phelps and watched him haul eight gold medals. My desire to emulate Phelps intensified to the point where I even imitated the way he spoke with his American accent! After seeing him in Beijing, I wanted to swim like Phelps.

In an interview at the Beijing Olympics, Phelps said that he did 1 000 m for his cool down after a race. That was now going to be my norm: after each race I did 1 000 m. There were times when the team would be waiting for me in the bus while I was on my cool down. If I had to attend a medal presentation, I would do my cool down afterwards. My teammates thought I was crazy and that it was too much – the norm was around 400 m: but if the best in the world was doing 1 000 m, then I was certainly not going to do anything less. My psychological adjustment to acquiring a champion mindset was taking shape, and part of this was to emulate the Phelps regime in every aspect.

By good fortune, I was selected to go to India for the 2008 Commonwealth Youth Games because one of the guys got injured. This event took place from 12 to 18 October. I was a wild card and, at 16, the youngest squad member in the team – the others were 18 – but Graham encouraged me. He told me it was going to be a big step up in terms of my competition levels and that I needed to make this adjustment. He explained that I couldn't go as I was: I would need to race and train harder in the mornings.

In the 200 m IM, I was in second position after the butterfly, and touched third. I had learnt from Phelps, who was the 'king of underwater', and I came off the wall fast to win in a time of 2:04.7. From that point, I began to compare my times with those of Phelps, who was the best in the world. His time for the 200 m IM was 1:54.5. I was 10 seconds behind him, and even though I had won this event, I knew that there was still a lot of room for improvement if I wanted to successfully compete with the likes of Phelps. I was not satisfied with where I was. I was determined to go faster.

For the 100 m backstroke, I made the final and finished sixth. In the 200 m breaststroke, however, I won the final, in lane 8, even though I had qualified last. I beat Kenneth To, the Australian swimmer, who came second in both the breaststroke events. Today, we are still great rivals. It was a good race – I came from the back of the field and clinched it from him in the last five metres. My time for the breaststroke was 2:21.00, a junior record.

Graham was extremely pleased with my performances (two golds – the other was for the 200 m IM – and one bronze, which I got for the 4 x 100 m relay) – all the more so as I had competed in my swimming trunks while the others all wore suits. And I hadn't even shaved, which helps save a few milliseconds. Graham's plan had simply been for me to do it for the experience. Then, a week or so later, I tore my groin muscle, which forced me to take time out from swimming. The injury was so severe that I couldn't train for breaststroke at all, and that is when I switched to butterfly. I knew it was a hard race, but I backed myself to make it if I put in the effort to win.

All said, the Commonwealth Youth Games provided a great experience for me to become exposed to the international scene. Usually, swimming is among the first events, so we had an extra few days to watch the other sports. The other memorable thing about the 2008 Indian Commonwealth Youth Games was how much curry I ate. Coming from Durban, I am no stranger to curry, but it was definitely a first for breakfast.

That year, after watching Phelps win eight gold medals in Beijing, I said to my dad that I was going to win the 200 m butterfly at the London Olympics. I was known for telling my dad certain things that seemed unrealistic at the time, but I have gone on to achieve them.

One of my first recorded times in the 200 m butterfly, at the end of 2008, was 2.02. The then South African champ was Wesley Gilchrist, the leader of our squad. I was closing in on Wes, and was around six seconds behind him. I told my dad I would beat him in the Natal Championships, but in the end I lost by one second to the winner, Riaan Schoeman. Wes came in second and I finished third. In a way, though, these weren't the ones I was chasing: my time of 2.02 put me 10 seconds behind Phelps and I was determined to get closer to him.

Dad understood my drive and determination, and he was supportive in my quest to be the best. He would wait patiently for me to finish my sessions. When everyone else was heading home, I would stay behind to practise my underwaters – the time that you can use dolphin or butterfly kicks below the surface after you have propelled yourself off the wall. This is restricted to 15 m after each turn and is harnessed by top swimmers to gain advantage. This was a key area and a necessary evil I needed to perfect if I was to improve my times. In the words of Muhammad Ali, 'I hated every minute of training, but I said, "Don't quit. Suffer now and live the rest of your life as a champion."'

Towards the end of 2008, I stayed away completely from breast-stroke, as I was afraid of aggravating my groin injury. I felt really stupid for causing the injury and, like I said, that was the last time I kicked a soccer ball. That injury was a sobering experience for me.

The banned swimsuit: breaking too many records?

In 2008, a controversy erupted in amateur and sponsored international competitive swimming with the introduction of full-body polyurethane swimming suits. At that point, I had never worn one of these extremely high-end products. The four most popular suits were the Arena X-Glide, the Speedo Lazer, the Blueseventy and the Jacket. These four suits changed the face of swimming: the swimmers who wore them broke nearly every world record.

The most controversial of the new suits was the one offered by Speedo, developed by Mectex, an Italian company, in association with the Australian Institute of Sport, and aided by Speedo's sponsored swimmers. The suit was partly developed at NASA's wind-tunnel testing facilities and used NASA's fluid-flow analysis software to support the design. Part of the focus of the suit was to allow for better oxygen flow to the muscles, and to hold the body in a more hydrodynamic position. It was able to achieve this by repelling water and thus increasing flexibility. The advanced technology didn't stop there, as the seams of the suit were ultrasonically welded to further reduce drag. The suit was also 100 per cent chlorine resistant, quick-drying and had internal compression panels. Speedo partnered with ANSYS, one of the world's leading engineering simulation software providers, in creating the suit. After testing, it was reported that these suits could lower a swimmer's racing times by 1.9 to 2.2 per cent, which led to critics of the suits dubbing their use as technological doping.

Nevertheless, the suit received the endorsement of FINA, the international governing body for water sports, for competitive use before the 2008 Beijing Olympics. Following its launch in February that year, 135 long- and short-course world records were broken. After the December 2008 European Short-Course Championships in Croatia, where 17 world records fell, it was felt there was a need to modify the rules surrounding swimsuits. The combined effects of the suit both compressing the body and trapping air for greater buoyancy meant that many competitors wore two, or even more, suits for increased effect. This led to critics claiming that, effectively, the new suits were providing an unfair advantage – much like the doping scandals that have dogged many sports. Therese Alshammar of Sweden was stripped of her world record in the 50 m butterfly because she was wearing two swimsuits.

Speedo was not the only manufacturer. German swimmer Britta Steffen was wearing the Adidas Hydrofoil when she slashed the 100 m freestyle world record in June 2008. She was quoted as saying that the suit made her feel like a 'speedboat' and that she felt no pain at the end of the race.

British Swimming's performance director, Michael Scott, advocated putting an asterisk next to world records that were achieved in polyurethane suits to distinguish them from records before and after their introduction. However, Mark Schubert, general manager of the US national team, said that the records should be stricken because they were artificially aided. 'I just don't think we've been good stewards of the sport to allow what's happened,' he said. However, Mark Schubert's boss, Chuck Wielgus, US Swimming's executive director, took a different stance, saying, 'I don't think we want to do anything to tarnish the performances of the athletes of the past.'

While FINA didn't nullify past records that had been set by athletes using polyurethane suits, the records were 'starred' in the same way that records set at high altitude are marked separately in the record books of track and field events.

FINA did, however, take notice of the complaints, and at its meeting in Dubai in March 2009, stipulated that swimsuits should not cover the neck, not extend past the shoulders and ankles, and that the suits' thickness and buoyancy should be limited. In a statement, FINA said it chose to deal with this situation by ruling on the lengths of swimsuits, rather than on their composition and structure. It seems as though the authorities were stumped as to what to do about the suits. The LZR Racer and all other Speedo Fast Skin competition suits were approved.

However, other suits, like the Blueseventy Nero Comp, were first banned then later unbanned.

The World Swimming Federation's decision to ban the suits from competitive events came amid calls from a number of national swimming federations for record-breaking suits to be banned. FINA then voted almost unanimously to reverse its previous policy and ban all body-length swimsuits. The decision was reversed partly because swimmers like Michael Phelps had threatened to withdraw from the sport competitively until the suits were outlawed. When the ban was effected, Phelps openly supported the decision. Phelps had worn the LZR Racer when he broke every one of the records in Beijing. But, in his favour, he did already hold those records before these suits were introduced.

In Rome, on 24 July 2009, during the World Aquatics Champ-ionships, FINA stated that their new policy was that men's swimsuits may only cover the area from the waist to the knee, and women's counterparts from the shoulder to the knee. They also stipulated that the fabric used must be a textile (i.e. a woven material) and that a suit may not have any fastening devices such as a zipper (drawstrings on male jammers are allowed). The new regulations took effect in January 2010.

With this ban, many of the current records may not be broken for many years to come. The return to standard textile suits – men in swimming shorts and women in suits from the knee to the shoulder strap – means that world records made in the hi-tech bodysuits will be almost impossible to better in the short term. Given that the ban is upheld by many top swimmers themselves, perhaps it is inevitable that it came about. Australian swimming star Libby Trickett told the BBC:

> It has taken the limelight from people's performances and that's not right. I don't think the sport should have headed in the direction it has, in terms of neoprene and polyurethane suits. I don't believe that is right for our sport at all and it's disappointing it's gone in that direction and it's disappointing that FINA allowed it to progress the way it did.

The UK's Rebecca Adlington, who won gold medals in the 400 m and 800 m freestyle events in Beijing, was also critical of the new swimsuits. 'I would never in a million years take a drug to help me, so why would I wear a suit just to improve my performance?' she told UK daily *The Telegraph*.

Another anti-bodysuiter, Franziska van Almsick, former world-record holder in the 200 m freestyle, told German newspaper *Der Tagesspiegel* how she vehemently opposed the 'full-body condom where all you see is the swimmer's face'.

The new swimsuits were manufactured from a very thin layer of foam-like material that enclosed tiny pockets of air, making its user far more buoyant than normal. As a result, the swimmer floated higher in the water and experienced less drag. The suits pushed water away from the swimmer's body and were therefore termed hydrophobic. The drag on the human body moving in water is around 780 times greater than when one is moving in air, so there was a considerable advantage gained by getting as much of the body above the water level as possible. These suits also made the body shape very smooth and hydrodynamic. Instead of the join between the body and the waist cord of the swimsuit adding extra drag, there was now a seamless, wrinkle-free, low-resistance outer shell skimming through the water. The downside was that putting on one of these suits took about half an hour. And they don't last long – they need to be replaced after a few races, and at about $500 (approximately R5 000) a time, that's expensive.

Perhaps the main disadvantage surrounding the bodysuits, however, was that not all swimmers wore them at championships, so there wasn't a level playing field. Those who wore them were entering a 'technological arms race', as different sponsoring companies tried to produce superior suits for their swimmers. The sponsorship deals that swimmers had signed prevented them from switching to a superior suit if it was made by a rival company.

I was a contender to qualify for the FINA World Championships to be held in Rome in 2009, and Graham was pressuring me to get a body-suit. Two days before the competition, we bought a second-hand one. I swam in the trials and qualified for the 400 m IM by 0.02 seconds. That booked me a place for the World Championships. At just 17, I was the youngest guy in the squad. It was a huge achievement for me and I was really pleased with myself. Let me put that suit into perspective – just by using it, my times from 2008 to 2009 improved by about five seconds. I achieved a time for the 200 m butterfly of 1.57, which qualified me for the World Championships.

I was finally going to race against my hero, Michael Phelps. After his phenomenal success at the Beijing Olympics, he was now an even bigger superstar.

Before participating in the July World Championships in Rome, I competed at Barcelona's Mare Nostrum event in June 2009. I swam a respectable race and was placed second in the 400 m IM. I didn't make the final in my two preferred events – the 400 m IM and the 200 m butterfly – but was placed in the top 20 in both. I felt that this wasn't a bad accomplishment for a 17-year-old in his first year of international competition at senior level.

At the World Championships, I was in awe of most of my competition – Phelps, Kaio de Almeida, Takeshi Matsuda and Ryan Lochte. These were all guys I looked up to. In the 400 m IM, I finished 16th (4:17.39); in the 200 m butterfly I came in 17th (1:56.90) and missed out on the semi-finals by 0.01 seconds. If I had qualified, I would have swum with Phelps in the semis in lane 8, with him in lane 4. That would have been a dream come true. But at least I got to watch Phelps live from the arena as part of the biggest crowd I've seen in my life for a swimming event, with around 20 000 in attendance. An important factor, and something that is key to my success, is watching my competitors. I learn a lot from analysing their races.

That event was the first time I had travelled with the South African senior team, my first national cap. One of the great experiences of the championship was taking part in the celebrations with teammate Cameron van der Burgh as he broke the world record in the 50 m breaststroke. Cam was the big gun in our team and we were all so proud of him. That moment, when he stood on the podium, is etched in my memory, and I was determined to climb on to that number-one spot for my country one day and hear our national anthem being sung.

At the end of 2009, I competed in the FINA-Arena Swimming World Cup, which featured the short course – a pool with 25 m laps. It was there that many of my critics started to take me seriously. This tournament was hosted in six countries and each event had the Olympic programme crammed into just two days, a schedule that enabled me to swim only in certain selected races. The host cities were Moscow, Stockholm, Tokyo, Beijing, Berlin and my home city of Durban. Overall, I won three golds, taking two in Durban and one in Berlin, and I also came away with three silver and three bronze medals.

I won the 400 m IM (Durban, Berlin) and the 200 m butterfly (Durban). In Berlin I produced what some regard as my most impressive performance of the year. While I didn't medal in the 200 m butterfly there, I did break the African record in my heat, and then I broke the African 400 m IM record when I won the final. However, personally, the greatest accomplishment of 2009 for me was when I got the bronze in the 200 m IM, in which I finished 0.58 seconds behind Michael Phelps in a race in which my compatriot, Darian Townsend, broke the world record. Darian had been part of the South African relay team that got gold at the 2004 Athens Olympics.

2010: Youth Olympics and Commonwealth Games

In a lot of ways, 2010 was the defining year for me. On 12 April 2010 I turned 18, which entitled me to vote and get my driver's licence. But apart from my coming of age, there was also some magic in the air. I guess it was the expectancy and the belief that I had it in myself to do well that year. It was the year of the Commonwealth Games in India, the Youth Olympics in Singapore and the World Short-Course Championships – lots of opportunities for me to stamp my mark in the swimming world.

I was really fortunate to compete in these three major events in one year. Not many people achieve this and I was still in my last year of school. Because it was going to be such a busy year for me, I spoke to the staff at school to see if I could extend my last year over two years. However, after weighing up my options, I decided to do it over the one year.

In January 2010, the controversial swimming suits were banned. This meant we had to train even harder to make up for the advantage they had provided in terms of buoyancy and the more streamlined profile.

Following my strong performances in 2009, I had offers for swimming scholarships in the US. After speaking to the people close to me, however, I decided to remain committed to my country, my coach and my beloved Seagulls Swimming Club in Durban. Going into 2010, my sights were set on increasing my medal haul at the upcoming Commonwealth Games in India, where, two years previously, at the Commonwealth Youth Games, I had won gold medals in the 200 m IM (setting a new record) and the 200 m breaststroke. Afterwards I would have to shift my focus to December's World Short-Course Championships in Dubai. Based on my improved performances in 2009, I was expecting to add to my medal tally in these events.

Qualifying for the Commonwealth Games, I swam the fourth-fastest 200 m butterfly in the world that year (1:56.86). That was in April at the South African nationals in Durban. But amid all the euphoria and celebrations, a piece of shocking news was about to hit me. Doctors had diagnosed my mother with breast cancer. My parents had known about this since January but had decided not to break the dreadful news to me then, as they did not want it to affect my chances of qualifying for the Commonwealth Games and the Youth Olympics.

They told me in April, after I had qualified. It was very difficult for me to process. The thought that my mum, whom I loved so much, could die from this terrible disease, brought about a mixed bag of emotions for me. On the one hand, in the public eye, I was now the South African national champ, set for the Commonwealth Games, but on another, personal level, I was facing the prospect that my mother was dying of cancer. Although it was really hard to endure these thoughts, Mum's courage in dealing with her cancer spurred me on. Having her there in the stands at the Youth Olympics watching me take part was so inspiring for me that I competed for her alone.

The Youth Olympics is an international multi-sport event, first held in Singapore from 14 to 26 August 2010. This event is the brainchild of Austrian Johann Rosenzopf, who proposed the concept in 1998. They are scheduled to be held every four years in staggered summer and winter events, consistent with the current Olympic Games format. The age bracket for the athletes is 14 to 18.

I was a medal favourite for this event and I expected to win more than one medal. The media was now heaping the pressure on, as the previous year I had done well in the World Cup.

My first race was the 400 m freestyle and an opportunity for my first medal was up for grabs. It was not a race that I usually swam, so when I finished second I was certainly not disappointed. It was a great result. In my next race, the 200 m freestyle, I knew I would do better, as it was shorter. This was an embarrassing swim for me because the pace was so slow that I never made the finals, even after touching first with a time of 1.52. I didn't want this to happen again, so I was well prepared for my next race, the 200 m IM.

I qualified for the final in lane 5, with another South African in lane 3, flanking the Commonwealth Youth Games winner, Kenneth To, in lane 4. As I dived in, I knew I had to swim hard and was determined to get the gold. I was relieved when I won with a time of 2.68 and received the gold medal, an experience made even sweeter when we sang our national anthem.

With the butterfly now my strongest stroke, I was expecting to consolidate my gold in the 200 m IM with another gold in the 100 m butterfly. In this race, however, I made the mistake of giving the eventual winner too much of a head start, and in the final turn I touched the wall seventh. That was too much of a lead and even though I finished strong, it was only good enough for second and a silver medal. I was not happy: I knew I could have got gold.

With the 4 x 100 m freestyle relay, it was an opportunity for us to make history for coach Graham Hill. He had coached the South African team that won the gold in Athens for this event, and this was the first Youth Olympics, so he had a chance to make history if his team won the race at the Olympics and the Youth Olympics in succession. We were pumped for this race and favourites to win, but, disappointingly, it was not to be. We faded to clinch the third spot.

I led the relay and was highly motivated because of my earlier second place in the 100 m butterfly. I gave the team a great start and achieved a personal best for my 100 m freestyle. It was neck and neck all the way, and there was nothing in it, although we did have a marginal lead most of the way. But Russia and China finished very strong. In the end, we were happy to get the bronze. I enjoy participating in relay, as it allows me to be part of a team.

Going into day five, I was really determined to win the 200 m butterfly, especially after finishing second in the 100 m. Ominously, in this event I was racing against Bence Pulai from Hungary, who had turned out to be my bogey. For some reason, in previous races he had always beaten me. We were in adjacent lanes, with me in lane 7. I also remember this race well because in the crowd I spotted four girls wearing T-shirts, each printed with a letter of my name, C-H-A-D. After the first 50 m, I touched first, likewise at 100 m, and Pulai and I were together at 150 m. I was watching him close in on me over that last lap, and as much as I tried, over the last 10 metres he was just too fast for me and he won the gold.

This race took place almost exactly two years before the main Olympics in London 2012. If I had won that race, I would have been the first person to have won the event at the Youth Olympics and not the

Olympics. It didn't happen, but, nevertheless, my time that day put me four seconds behind Michael Phelps – so I was improving all the time.

I walked away from the first Youth Olympics with a medal haul of one gold, three silvers and a bronze. My experience in Singapore was fantastic. I got to face the media more often and, again, it was a chance to compete with the best in the world – factors that were very important for my preparation for London 2012.

Boarding the plane to Delhi for the 2010 Commonwealth Games with the rest of the South African senior national swimming team was a huge high for me. I roomed with the breaststroke world champion, Cameron van der Burgh, and we became good friends. However, staying in the athletes' village with Cameron, Natalie du Toit and Roland Schoeman made me feel a bit like I was a junior rugby player getting to run on with the likes of Bryan Habana and Morné Steyn. The previous year, I had been the new guy so I had had to carry everyone's bags. But this year my initiation was complete: I was a fully-fledged member of the team.

Despite the negative publicity about the athletes' accommodation at the 2010 Commonwealth Games in Delhi, everything was in order in my view. There were reports from some of the athletes that the accommodation was not up to par and that some of the rooms were dirty. The only bad thing I can recall, however, was the snake that they found in Natalie's room – a four-metre cobra, which was pretty hair-raising.

On 4 October, I competed in the 200 m butterfly and came up against my fellow countryman Sebastian Rossouw, who had been the South African 200 m butterfly champion the previous year. He had finished sixth in the World Championships, so he was well established as a competent swimmer. Before this race, the outcome was reported as being wide open because the current world number two, Nick D'Arcy, had, astonishingly, failed to qualify. D'Arcy had been the favourite for the event after having performed well in the Pan Pacific Swimming Championships in August, to finish second to Michael Phelps. He had missed out qualifying for this final by just six-hundredths of a second. Readers may remember Nick D'Arcy for the wrong reasons – he was banned from the Australian team after assaulting a fellow swimmer before the 2008 Olympics. This resulted in him sitting out the Beijing Olympics and the World Championships in Rome 2009.

Going into this race, I was a bundle of nerves. This was going to be the first event of the Games where I was in contention for a medal and we had carefully planned the approach to achieve it. I had to make the final turn in the top three, then go hard out. But when the race began, everything went wrong because everyone started very fast. This meant I had to change my game plan in the middle of the race.

England's Michael Rock led at the 100 m and 150 m marks. I let him lead most of the way and when we got to the 150 m mark, I had moved up to second when I touched for the last 50 m. I noticed he was starting to tire, and I slowly began to reel him in. Before the last turn, I took a couple of breaths, hit the wall hard and went for it, and I finished very strong, winning with a time of 156.48 seconds – a new Commonwealth Games record. When I looked up to see my name on the board, I went wild. It was huge for me – everything I had worked for, all the sacrifices, made sense at that moment. It was also South Africa's first Commonwealth Games gold medal in Delhi, and that gold medal was my first in a senior major competition. And, to top it all, I had beaten the Games record in the 200 m butterfly event, set by New Zealand's Moss Burmester at the Melbourne Games four years ago.

Michael Rock held on for silver while Canada's Stefan Hirniak got the bronze. Sebastian ended up finishing eighth.

Interestingly, when I watch this race again, I notice that the commentators don't mention my name once – until I touch for home, hit the underwater, and only when I come up do you hear them say: 'It's Chad le Clos and look at that great turn by Chad ... is he going to do it?'

To answer their question, 'Yes, I did it.' One of the South African newspapers was perhaps more indulgent in describing my performance: 'But the day belonged to Le Clos, who recently excelled at the Youth Olympics. Le Clos was as lethal in Delhi, as he excelled over the last 50 metres to pull away and secure a South African gold on day one.'

After my win in the 200 m butterfly, I went into the 400 m IM with a lot more confidence. This took place on day four. I led from the front to finish in first place – my second gold of the Games. Graham had said from the outset that I would win this event and he was right. He played a big role in how we tackled this race. I clocked 4:13.25, which put me in seventh place in the world rankings. I was really charged up for this race and surged ahead from the first stroke of the butterfly. I had to stamp my authority right from the get-go, especially as the butterfly was my strong stroke. Swimming the butterfly so hard in that first leg set me up beautifully for the remaining backstroke, breaststroke and freestyle.

Canada's Brian Johns tried to catch me in the backstroke leg with Australia's Thomas Fraser-Holmes, but they fell off the pace during the breaststroke. At one stage, South Africa was first and second as Riaan Schoeman moved into contention over the breaststroke leg, but he dropped out of it during the freestyle leg. All my effort paid off with the rampant pace I had set, and I got home in a new Commonwealth Games best of 4:14.25. England's Joe Roebuck held off my teammate Riaan Schoeman for the silver spot, with Riaan grabbing the bronze, having fought off a late challenge from Welshman Thomas Haffield. I hadn't ever previously beaten Riaan in this event and it all went according to plan. I had surprised not only myself, but also my teammates. The atmosphere afterwards was electrifying and I received lots of SMSes from back home, which lifted my confidence even more.

I got two bronze medals in the relays – for the men's 4 x 200 m free-style relay and the 4 x 100 m freestyle relay. I took the silver for the 4 x 100 medley, swimming the butterfly third leg. Graham Hill was extremely happy with our overall performance and said: 'This shows where we are as we start the build-up to London 2012. There is a new generation coming through and there is a whole group of even younger swimmers queuing behind them so I am really excited about the future.' Graham has always taught me to experience as much as I can from competitions and learn from the experience.

Looking back at Delhi 2010, I was pleasantly surprised by the event and the venue, despite the negative media reports in the run-up. The training facilities, about a kilometre from where we were staying, were excellent. There was an outdoor pool with a roof, similar to the one we had trained in at the Youth Olympics in Singapore. The competition pool was indoor and air-conditioned. My room-mate, Cameron van der Burgh, our country's flag bearer at Delhi 2010, helped me settle down, and taught me how to deal with the media and stay relaxed.

On our return to Durban, the weather was not very welcoming – dark skies and clouds threatening rain. But the welcome at King Shaka International Airport was a very pleasant surprise: waiting for me as I walked into the arrivals hall were about 300 Westville Boys High students greeting me with the sounds of Zulu war cries. I was close to tears with emotion, a flashback to how I had felt when I received my first gold at the Commonwealth Games with *Nkosisikelel' iAfrika* playing. Seeing my family and friends sent shivers down my spine.

After my success at Delhi 2010, people thought that I was living an abnormal life. To put the record straight, the following is an overview of my weekly regime back then (one that is fairly normal for an athlete):

Monday

4:15 a.m.	Wake up; have two cups of coffee; perhaps some Future Life.
4:50–6:45 a.m.	Training with Graham Hill's Seagulls Club at the Lahee Park pool, Pinetown.
7:15 a.m.	Rush from Pinetown to school in Westville.
7:30 a.m.–2:50 p.m.	School. Try to squeeze in a protein shake and some multivitamins.
3:15–5 p.m.	Back to the pool for more training.
5:15 p.m.	Extra land work.
6 p.m.	Head home with best mate and training partner, Leith Shankland, for a game of Fifa on Playstation.
7:30 p.m.	Dinner.

Tuesday

4:15 a.m.	Wake up; coffee and a bite to eat.
4:50–6:45 a.m.	Training with the squad at Lahee Park pool.
7:30–9 a.m.	Physio.
9 a.m.–2:50 p.m.	School.
3:15–5 p.m.	Back to the pool for more training.
5:15–6 p.m.	Extra land work.
6:30 p.m.	Tuesday is family dinner day, usually with my older brother and sister. Dad normally cooks something like a chicken curry, lentils or oxtail.

Wednesday

4:15 a.m.	Wake up; coffee; Future Life.
4:50–6:45 a.m.	Training with Seagulls at Lahee Park pool.
7:15 a.m.	To school in Westville.
7:30 a.m.–2:50 p.m.	School. Occasionally, I will be fetched for physio.

12:30 p.m. and afterwards	Go for a steak or chops with my dad.
3:15–5 p.m.	Back to the pool for more training.
5:15–6 p.m.	Extra land work.
6 p.m.	Head home with Shanky for a game of Fifa on Playstation.
7:30 p.m.	Dinner.
Thursday	
4:15 a.m.	Wake up; coffee and a bite to eat.
4:50–6:45 a.m.	Training with the squad at the Lahee Park pool.
7:30–9 a.m.	Physio.
9 a.m.–2:50 p.m.	School. Lunch might be a couple of fresh bread rolls and some Hungarian salami or other cold meats.
3:15–5 p.m.	Back to the pool for more training.
5:15–6 p.m.	Extra land work.
7:30 p.m.	Supper – usually biggest meal of the day.
Friday	
4:15 a.m.	Wake up; coffee; Future Life.
4:50–6:45 a.m.	Training with Seagulls Club at the Lahee Park pool.
7:15 a.m.	To school in Westville.
7:30 a.m.–2:50 p.m.	School. Occasionally our weekend galas start on a Friday, so I need to prepare for late afternoon/ evening races.
Weekends	Often compete in galas on Saturdays and Sundays.

For those of you keen to go the extra mile, here is a training regime called the Hungarian set. Usually on a Saturday morning, I would do the following 14 x 400 m sets in the following order (make sure you prepare yourself adequately before attempting these):

4 x 100 m butterfly; 400 m IM; 4 x 100 m freestyle; 4 x 100 m back-stroke; 400 m IM; 4 x 100 m freestyle; 400 m freestyle; 4 x 100 m breaststroke; 4 x 100 m freestyle; 400 m freestyle; 4 x 100 m freestyle; 400 m IM; 4 x 100 m freestyle; 400 m freestyle.

This was my training schedule after Delhi 2010, when I was in my last year of school. With no more school, can you imagine what it is like now?

It's good to have a dream, but to achieve it takes hard work. I was under no illusions that to beat Michael Phelps or to dominate swimming in the way he did, I was going to have to make a lot of sacrifices. I set my mind to achieving this and knew that to be a champion, I had to train like one. There are no short cuts to the top and I was mentally prepared to go the extra mile and do whatever my coach expected of me.

5 Family crisis, matric exams and the FINA World Championships

'I was now closing in on Phelps – only about two seconds away from the world's best.'

In 2010, the public may have been able to see that I was enjoying great success in the pool, but what they were not aware of was the fact that my mum had cancer, nor the effect this had on me. These were very trying times for my family, but I was able to draw strength and courage from my mum. Despite her fight with the illness, she remained strong and positive throughout. She never complained and when I asked her how she was, she would always say she felt good.

In early 2010, Mum had discovered a lump in her breast. On that Friday we had planned a family picnic at the Midmar Dam but she didn't tell anyone, as she felt that she did not want to alarm any of us. However, she made an appointment for a check-up with the doctor the following week. The results of a test confirmed, in her words, many a woman's worst fear: breast cancer, the most common form of cancer among women globally. She had a 2 cm lump, but, fortunately, it had been detected in its early stages. She decided to keep the news from me to allow me to focus on qualifying for the Commonwealth Games without the distraction of worrying about her. The doctor told her that the cancer was at a very early stage, so it would not pose a problem if she waited a little while to break the news to me.

She told us later that her immediate thoughts were that she was going to die and a type of panic set in. However, my mother is not the sort of person to be negative, and quickly realised that she had to be strong. Those who have had the same battle will tell you that it is not easy to remain positive in the face of a disease that might kill you. One of the first things she did was to find out more about her 'enemy'. I always like to study my opposition, and Mum says she adopted a similar ploy.

After I had qualified in April for the Commonwealth Games, Mum broke the news. You can imagine how gutted I was. However, I wanted to remain positive in the hope that she would overcome it, so I held on to the good news that the cancer was in the very early stages and therefore the chances of her beating it were high. As an ambassador for the Cancer Association of South Africa (CANSA), I learnt that it is advisable for women to check themselves regularly. It was greatly inspiring for me to know that my mother was going to be in Singapore to watch me compete at the Youth Olympics in August.

Mum had a lumpectomy in May and the prognosis was good: there were no cancerous cells in the glands – it was localised to the breast tissue – so she didn't need a mastectomy and began radiation treatment in June. She underwent 30 radiation treatments over a period of six weeks – so that was five times a week. The radiation was successful and she received the all-clear to go to Singapore. A side effect of the radiation was that it caused her skin to flake off.

If having to endure cancer weren't bad enough, on the last day of her treatment we got the terrible news that my mum had lost her mother. That really knocked her down. Losing her mother was worse than the cancer, she told us at the time. My grandmother died on 4 August from an aneurysm while I was in Singapore. Mum didn't tell me that she had passed away, as she did not want me to lose my focus. Before she could leave for Singapore, she arranged the funeral and came to join me on 8 August.

At the time, we couldn't afford for both my parents to come to Singapore, so Mum came alone, as she was able to arrange her accommodation with one of our team's swimmer's mothers, who lived in Singapore. She says:

Being there to see Chad win those medals was a real bittersweet moment for me. I had just lost my mum and I was fighting cancer, but I was so happy for Chad's success. He told me that he would be swimming for me and being there to see him win made me so proud. It was so overwhelming that it brought tears to my eyes.

Chad's success at the Youth Olympics was even more notable, given how he had to overcome the stress of knowing I was ill. During my treatment, Chad was at the Commonwealth Games and as soon as he returned he had to get on with his studies, as it was his last year of high school. During that time, I didn't want his routine to change; I wanted to keep things as normal as possible, and not upset his training and swimming routines.

Mum could not attend the Commonwealth Games because of her treatment. But she says that for my 200 m butterfly final, she left work early to watch it with her cousin. She was so nervous that she couldn't bring herself to watch me live on the TV, and had to turn away. When her cousin started jumping up and down and shouting, she turned to the screen just in time to see me finishing first. I had told Mum that I would be competing for her. 'Knowing Chad was swimming for me was such a boost at the time and a welcome distraction from all the treatment I was having,' she says.

Mum started chemotherapy in August and she says it took a lot out of her:

It seems no amount of information from the medical team is enough to prepare you for what you experience during chemo. Chemotherapy treatment for breast cancer isn't used to destroy the tumour. Rather, the goal is to destroy any undetectable disease that may have spread beyond the breast. However, from my own experience, I can say that it is different for everybody. This is a very important point. Please don't be scared by the horror stories of others. I do admit that the thought of chemo can be frightening, especially if you don't like needles or the sight of blood, but once I became familiar with the procedure, I found it wasn't as bad as I had expected. My advice is to take all the horror stories with a pinch of salt and remain positive that you can beat cancer. It is true that some people suffer nausea, pain or fatigue, but there are just as many cancer patients who experience these side effects only minimally.

Dad is a bit of a master chef and we always enjoy his great cuisine, so it was a real shame that the chemotherapy made Mum lose her sense of taste and appetite – it temporarily destroys the taste buds. On her first day of chemo treatment, Mum says that she was looking forward to a good fillet steak, but was disappointed when, after Dad had prepared it for her, she found that she didn't have an appetite. Even Dad's famous chicken fillet and pasta no longer appealed to her. Surprisingly, though, she did have a taste for broccoli. 'My husband, Bert, was to use his famous word "unbelievable", and was very supportive, and made whatever I felt like eating,' she says.

The good news is that Mum's sense of taste returned, and she was able to enjoy Dad's cooking again.

After Mum's second chemo treatment, her hair began to fall out. This was a highly traumatic experience for her and the whole family. Every time she showered, her hair would fall out in clumps. It got so frustrating that she decided to have a short haircut. But that did not help much, as her hair continued to fall out everywhere. She decided enough was enough, and shaved it all off. As her child, it was not nice for me to see Mum go through this. 'No woman wants to lose her hair,' she says. 'My hair used to be long and I would often get complimented for it. Women will know what I am talking about – even the Bible says something to the effect that "a woman's hair is her glory". So you can imagine how devastated I was to lose it. I asked Bert to bring the clippers, as I needed to shave my hair out of necessity. The whole house was in tears, and Bianca, feeling my pain, offered to shave my hair off. As she shaved my hair, there was a solemn mood in the whole house. However, as emotional as it was, I felt it was a small price to pay for a bigger victory.'

Mum then asked one of her friends to buy her two wigs. However, she didn't like the wigs and they made her feel hot. So, instead, she chose to wear her loss of hair with pride instead of disguising it by wearing a wig. She says that she realised that her hair loss was beyond her control, something that she had to accept and nothing to be ashamed of: 'I can remember one time walking through a shopping mall with Chad. He said to me, reassuringly, "Hey, Mum, you got cancer." It was the way that he said it, as if to say that everything would turn out okay. He always said that I looked good, which is very reassuring and encouraging to hear for someone in my situation.'

You may feel that you have never needed anyone to accompany you to the doctor, so why should it be different with cancer? However, cancer is much more complicated, and the information presented to the patient can be overwhelming. Mum says that having Dad with her to take notes, hold her hand and even just to talk to the doctor when she was not in a state to, made a big difference. Dad made her laugh at the chemo treatment sessions and had the team in stitches with his antics. Mum's chemo programme ended in the first week of December. She says that she was grateful that Dad had accompanied her to each session. Her hair started growing back after the treatment ended and she was glad to return to some normality. On the last day of her treatment, I left for the World Championships in Dubai, where I was competing. For her last session, she asked her niece, Angie, to make her some cupcakes so that

Mum could show her appreciation to the nursing staff and doctors who had taken such good care of her.

My mother received the all-clear in March 2011. Since then, she has had regular check-ups. She says, 'Being a positive person, I believe that my experience with cancer is an opportunity to make other people aware that they need to take heed of their body and the changes within it. You can always overcome your obstacles with a positive attitude.'

When I collected the South African Sports Awards (SASA) Newcomer of the Year award in 2011, in my acceptance speech I dedicated it to women who had breast cancer, and especially to my mother. As a result of my experience with Mum's fight with cancer, I decided to become an ambassador for CANSA, a non-profit organisation that offers an integrated service to the public and everyone affected by cancer by means of research, education and support. It's my way of giving something back in return for the meaningful work that the association does. My role as ambassador entails making appearances at CANSA events and functions that I am invited to, donating some of my kit or speaking at events to raise awareness of the great work that they do. I also dedicate a portion of my earnings to CANSA.

At the Stockholm leg of the 2011 World Cup, I swam in a pink cap and swimsuit as a token of support to my mother and other cancer sufferers. The Swim for CANSA project was launched in conjunction with one of my sponsors, Arena, as part of the global Breast Cancer Awareness Month in October 2011. Arena designed the specially made pink swim cap and suit that I wore at the Stockholm event.

My role at CANSA was received positively by Lucy Balona, the organisation's spokesperson, who acknowledged my support and added: 'For Chad, the fight against breast cancer is a personal one. With his image and association, we can reach many more supporters and friends who can join our community fighting cancer and spreading hope to those affected by cancer.'

Giuseppe Musciacchio, the general manager of brand development at my sponsor, Arena, said, 'We had no hesitation in joining Chad in this worthy cause. Here at Arena we believe that we have an obligation to go beyond the pool to support those less fortunate than us, those whose lives are difficult and challenging. As a result, we're more than willing to give support to our Elite Team members in their efforts to "give back".'

Final exams

When I returned home after the 2010 Commonwealth Games, I needed to focus on my studies to complete my last year of high school. I had two weeks to prepare for my matric exams. I didn't want to succeed only in the pool, so I made sure I allocated sufficient time to studying. I got a lot of help and extra tuition from my teachers, and especially from my buddy, the brainy Leith Shankland.

Of all my school subjects, I particularly liked history. I enjoy how the subject sheds light on other cultures and peoples – especially as I travel so much around the world. Travelling is also one of the best ways to learn about people and different cultures. I have had the privilege of visiting many countries. For me, one of the most amazing places is India. It is a vast country with a highly diverse culture, as there are around 1.2 billion people. I spend about two-and-a-half months a year in Europe because of swimming events, and studying European history has helped me understand the traditions that have gone into shaping and forming the continent.

I believe that being aware of our local history is crucial to understanding the dynamics of the society in which we live. We should be proud of our history. In South Africa we have had to overcome so much to be where we are today, and we should celebrate great national heroes like Nelson Mandela and others who sacrificed so much for all South Africans.

I was born two years before the democratic South Africa came into existence, so I was too young to have had any personal experience of what happened in the apartheid days, but, thanks to studying history, I have a good understanding of that defining era of South Africa's history. I can write quickly and it doesn't take me long to learn new things – I don't mess around. When it's time for learning, I learn; when it's time for work, I work; and, of course, when it's time for playing, I play. As much as I loved history, the most important subjects for me at school were mathematics and science, and I put a lot of effort into mastering them.

In matric I had to study very hard for Afrikaans because it is not my home language. By putting my effort into the Afrikaans literature paper, I managed to make up for the language papers, where I was weaker.

My swimming commitments and school work linked because the main thing that school and swimming taught me was the need for discipline.

It seems harsh when you are a child, but you soon appreciate discipline later in life. I would start training at 5 a.m., then go to school, go back to training at 3 p.m. and finally get home at 5:30 p.m. It was like the disciplined routine of a working life from the age of 15. Until I was 15, swimming had been more fun and recreational, but then I started training with the 'big boys' and from then on it was more like a discipline, a form of career.

This taught me that discipline is not all 'bad'. If you really want to achieve anything, you need to make sacrifices. Some of the sacrifices I have had to make have been not spending time in the company of friends. And I never really had holidays or went away with my parents because of training commitments. My little brother, Jordan, is now experiencing the same thing with his swimming.

I had good relationships with my teachers and our respect is mutual. I appreciate all they did for me. I still keep in regular contact with Trevor Hall, the principal of Westville Boys High. I caught up with Mr Hall recently and asked him to share a few words about my school days. He told me that what struck him was that nothing seemed to get me down:

Chad had no apparent feelings of insecurity and always had a positive outlook on life. In Grade 8, I noticed this particular trait in him. He had a very strict science teacher and, one day, she was berating him and three other boys. The others were clearly upset – but not Chad. He seemed comfortable – not disturbed by the telling-off they were getting. He has an easy-going manner. Maybe that is his way of handling pressure.

The principal always took an interest in my swimming:

Watching Chad in the school swimming galas was a real treat, as he would see to it that we would win by huge margins. This was mainly thanks to his explosive finishes. Coming from behind and winning is what Chad has been doing since his school days.

From the results he was achieving in the pool, it was evident that he was immensely talented, but he never portrayed himself as being better than anyone else. And he supported others, even in the other sports, and would turn up to their games and cheer them on. When he came back to school with his gold and silver medals from the

Olympics, he went to support our first XV rugby team. He didn't have to do that, but that's Chad for you – a humble motivator with an engaging personality.

Having got to know the Le Clos family, I can confidently say that Chad's parents have been crucial to his success. Bert has the dominant personality while Geraldine is the rock of the family, and I think they all rely a lot on her for her reliability and support. Her cancer affected Chad but he stayed strong and it was a great joy to him when she came through it.

Somehow, I managed to balance the huge swimming commitments with my school work in my final year. At least that's what the principal says:

Even when he was busy with training and competing around the world, when he got back to school he engaged with his work and made sure that he caught up with what he had missed out. In his crucial Grade 11 and 12 years, he spent a lot of time away, but always made the effort to go through past exam papers, so he was never too far off the pace. I am sure that it was not easy for him, with all the travelling he was doing. All credit to Chad for using his time productively and focusing on his academic duties when he needed to: he achieved three As in matric.

That historic night as we watched him swim in the Olympics, we knew Chad had a chance of a medal, but when he touched, like many other people, I didn't think he had won. His gold medal captivated the imagination of the whole school and this was evident when he came back to visit us afterwards.

From Chad's achievements we can all see the power of having a vision, and the hard work that he put in has made it a reality. We can all learn from him, and learn how to always finish strong in all aspects of our lives.

During the matric exams, I methodically broke the papers down into thirds and watched the time carefully. Again, this is the same strategy I use in training. I need to know my training set before I start, and prepare myself for it. So if we are doing a big freestyle set, I know that I need to stretch accordingly for that stroke before starting. Correct preparation is crucial for success. You cannot just turn up and expect to turn it on. This

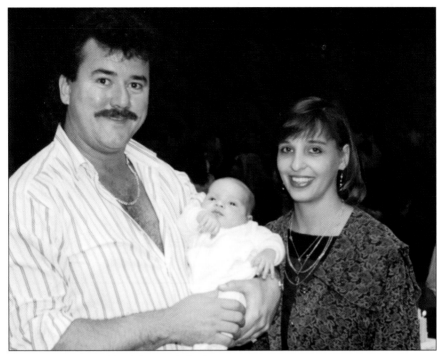

My proud parents with their cute baby boy.

Mum's favourite pic of me as a boy.

Chad the 'cow person': with one of my favourite childhood animals.

Proudly posing with my first surfboard.

Graham-Topfoto

When I ride the waves all the pressure disappears. I love to surf!

Told you I was no slouch in soccer. Here I am receiving my end-of-season trophy.

I developed a taste for winning gold at an early age. My competitive nature was encouraged and nurtured by my dad and has clearly stood me in good stead.

Me and Ms Manthey (right), my first swimming coach. Ms Manthey put me and my parents in contact with my coach of fourteen years, Graham Hill. I don't think that even she knew what an amazing journey that would take me on.

I'm a die-hard Man U fan.

The years I spent playing soccer as a boy were some of the best. Does the name of the team's sponsor on our jerseys look familiar?

Me and baby Jordan. I was a very proud big brother.

Penzance Primary School: I am 12 years old in this photo, which was taken to show me off as the top-seeded under-12 swimmer in KwaZulu-Natal and South Africa. My dream to become an Olympic star was strengthened by my achievements as a young swimmer.

Westville Boys' High School Photography Task Team

Crowd surfing: I received a hero's welcome from boys at the high school I attended, Westville Boys High School, when I visited them after winning the gold at the Olympics.

Mariclair Smit

The Chad le Clos Pool named in my honour at Westville Boys High School. Here I am with WBHS principal Trevor Hall.

Danie and Jacques Marais

Me with my teammates and friends: Dave Rankin, Ryan Passmore, Leith 'Shanky' Shanklin, Ayrton Sweeney, Graig Getz, Danie Marais and Ashley Oliver. These guys have been there for me through the best and the worst.

Jacques Naude (Independant Newspapers)

With my family. You can't see my brother-in-law, Pedro, in this photo because he's taking the shot.

methodical approach has been key to everything I have done. If I was away from school because of swimming, I would make a plan to apply myself to a major school project that I may have missed.

This type of planning and discipline also has a psychological aspect. In June 2012, before the Olympics, I knew that I had to be away from home for three months, so I prepared myself for it mentally well in advance. In January 2012, I began making the psychological adjustments and mental preparations for what was to come and how I was going to deal with it. On tour, I could see how some of the other guys battled with being away from their family and partners, and it did affect their performance negatively because they were not prepared. Whatever it is you do, you must be 100 per cent prepared, otherwise you won't achieve the best of it.

2010 FINA World Short-Course Championships, Dubai

After completing my exams, I was back into focusing full-on for my next event, the World Championships in Dubai. Most people said that my performance at the Commonwealth Games was my best in 2010, but I beg to differ: I think it was my performance in Dubai because it came straight after the pressure of my final exams and I faced world-class opposition there.

This event was the tenth World Short-Course Championships, staged in a 25 m pool, from 15 to 19 December 2010. It was held at the Dubai Sports Complex. In Dubai, American Ryan Lochte became the first swimmer to win seven medals at a short-course world championship. Lochte won all five of his individual events and six of his eight events overall. He failed to win a medal in just one event – the 400 m freestyle relay on the opening night, when he finished fourth. And to highlight the level of his performance, in two of his events – the 200 and 400 m IMs – Lochte set world records, the only individual world records in 2010 since the high-tech bodysuit ban had come into effect at the start of the year.

On day six of the event, I qualified second for the 200 m butterfly. For the finals, I was going to be up against some tough competition – firstly, the Hungarian László Cseh, who had represented his country at the 2008 Olympics in Beijing in three swimming events: the 400 m IM, the 200 m butterfly and the 200 m IM. Despite setting the European record in all of these races, Cseh took the silver medal in each, finishing second behind Michael Phelps, who won each event with a new world record. In both

IMs, Cseh came out ahead of the bronze medal winner, Ryan Lochte.

Another formidable opponent I was up against in this race was the Brazilian Kaio Márcio de Almeida. In the finals of the Stockholm step of the World Short-Course Championships, in November 2009, De Almeida had set a world record in the short-course 200 m butterfly at 1:49.11.

With competition like this, people did not expect me to get a medal, let alone win. But you probably know me better – I always believe I can beat anyone. In the final, I beat the world-record holder, De Almeida, by 0.05 of a second and Cseh, the Olympic silver medallist, by 0.11 of a second. People say it was a very narrow victory, but, again, it was all down to the planning and execution. The tactic we employed for this race would form the blueprint for my all-important London 2012 race. I sat just off the leaders, allowing me to finish strongly, powering from fourth to first to get the gold in 1:51.56. I became the youngest world champion of the short-course 200 m butterfly event.

Even though I had won my three gold medals in the 2009 FINA World Cup in Rome, this win in Dubai was more special because of the high calibre of the opposition I raced against. Don't get me wrong, the 2009 gold medals were also great, but in regard to the world rankings of the field I was racing against, I regard my Dubai win as my first real major title.

My swimming-club colleague Luke Pendock was in the stands with the rest of the South African supporters and recalls the event:

For the 200 m butterfly, I was with the rest of the South African team next to Chad's dad, Bert. Chad was in lane 5 and for the last 25 m was lying in fifth or sixth position and quite far back. At that stage, you would not have thought he was in medal contention. But then he turned on his magic in the final turn with another brilliant underwater, coming from nowhere to catch up with the others. When he finally touched the wall, we didn't think he had won. There was a slight pause before his name came up as the winner: Chad had won the gold. It was his first major world title. Bert dropped into his seat shouting, 'My son is a lion.' The South African squad and supporters went hysterical. I waited around for him after the race, as he had to do a drugs test first, but I couldn't get near Chad because by then he was mobbed by supporters.

Doping in swimming

Luke mentioned that, at the end of the race, I had to be tested for drugs. This is something I fully endorse to help keep our sport clean. I would hate swimming to slip to the lows that cycling reached with the Lance Armstrong debacle. Illegal performance boosters have been used for as long as sports have been around, and this will probably continue unless strict measures are taken to curb their use. Swimming has also had its problems with doping. It is now known that some of the former East German swimmers were systematically using banned substances. At the time, many of the swimmers did not really understand what they were being made to take (the team doctors, managers and coaches were suspects with these interventions) – but they do now. If you look at the pattern of medals won by East German female swimmers in the Olympics over a period of two decades, it is evident that something dubious was occurring:

Number of East German Olympic swimming medallists in the period 1964–1988

Year	Total number of medals won	Golds
1964	0	0
1968	6	2
1972	5	0
1976	18	11
1980	26	11
1984 (boycotted event)	N/A	N/A
1988	22	10

When the Berlin Wall came down, and East and West Germany were unified, the doping records were found, doctors and sports directors were taken to court and the sad, brutal doping stories became public. However, no one was stripped of their medals by the IOC.

Chinese competitive swimmers were also exposed for doping. The team went from nothing to four golds at the 1992 World Championships and the 1992 Olympics, and to 12 golds at the 1994 World Championships. That kind of improvement in performance raised too many eyebrows, so at the 1994 Asian Games, the Chinese team came under scrutiny and 11 of their women swimmers tested positive for dihydrotestosterone. At the 1996 Olympics, they only won a single gold medal and, to their credit, none of them tested positive. However, in the 1998 World Championships, four swimmers tested positive, and human growth hormone (HGH) was found in breaststroker Yuan Yuan's luggage. Before the 2000 Olympics, China removed four women from its squad for odd test results and no swimmer from China won any medals. At the 2004 Olympics, none of the swimmers tested positive and they earned one gold medal. China doesn't have a very good record, with more than 40 Chinese swimmers since 1990 having failed drug tests.

In its objective to eradicate doping from swimming, credit has to go to FINA, which has been very robust in helping ensure that our sport remains drug-free. London 2012 saw the most extensive anti-doping programme ever established at the Olympic Games. There were over 6 200 tests carried out on both urine and blood. Each medallist and four other athletes from every final were subjected to testing.

The front line in doping now concerns high-impact, hard-to-trace substances such as the blood booster erythropoietin (EPO), synthetic testosterone and HGH. The World Anti-Doping Agency (WADA) identified these three substances as the greatest threat to integrity on the eve of the Games, but catching those who use them requires vigilance, luck and resources. All three are similar to naturally occurring substances and can be detected only in a limited time frame by means of blood tests, which are more expensive and invasive than urine testing. The window for detection is short. EPO is detectable only for a matter of days after administration. There is a new test for HGH that has increased its window for detection, but only to weeks.

Under the WADA code, a document harmonising anti-doping policies in all sports and all countries, WADA has an obligation to coordinate anti-doping activities and to provide a mechanism to assist stakeholders with their implementation of the code.

Swimmers also have to adhere to the so-called Whereabouts Programme, whereby athletes are accountable for submitting their exact location for every hour between 6 a.m. and 11 p.m. This is somewhat inconvenient, but I totally support it if it helps to eliminate cheats. I have integrated this inconvenience into my life and most athletes acknowledge that it's a necessary step towards a clean sport and a level playing field.

The Whereabouts Programme requires competitive athletes to confirm their exact location to the relevant testing authority for one hour a day, seven days a week, 365 days a year. This needs to be done quarterly and can be adjusted as circumstances change.

The information that needs to be submitted is a primary residential address; training locations, dates and times; any temporary addresses (e.g. during holidays); flight information (flight number, and departure and arrival times); competition locations, dates and accommodation details; and a specific 60-minute time slot and location. During the 60-minute time slot, the athlete is required to be available for testing at a nominated location. If you need to change this, you can do so right up until the start of the 60-minute time slot and you must stay at the designated location for the whole of the 60 minutes.

Although it does seem intrusive and inconvenient, I support this intervention, and I reiterate that it is necessary. Recently, my dad and I were preparing to go out for dinner with former Manchester United and South African footballer, Quinton Fortune, when I got the call from WADA to present myself for a test. It was 8 p.m. and I was on holiday in England. No sweat; I just had to call Quinton and explain that we would be late.

Even though I had established myself as a swimmer to be reckoned with in 2010, at the start of 2011 I felt what most teenagers experience when they finish school – indecision. Swimming is unlike the big-money sports like rugby and soccer, where, if you show promise, you can land a contract that pays well. So, at the beginning of 2011, I was faced with the decision of whether I should pursue a tertiary education or not. I decided to postpone my tertiary studies and pursue my swimming career. Professional swimming is very demanding, and I knew that I could always continue with my studies after my swimming career. The converse – taking a break from swimming at that point and then trying to revive it after three or four years – would have been incredibly difficult, especially with the momentum I had achieved and my improving performance. The physical demands of swimming are greater than with other sports, mainly because you are competing in a different medium – water. So if you don't maintain the same intensity level, it creates a huge mountain to encounter later on when you attempt to get back into it. My parents and I discussed this at length and they both supported me in my decision.

As I reflect, 2011 got off to a bit of a slow start in terms of swimming and it was a bit harder to get going. This could have been because 2010 had put me on a swimming high with the Youth Olympics and Commonwealth Games, and I also experienced a low as a result of my mother's cancer.

2011 FINA Long-Course World Championships

The FINA Long-Course World Championships were held in Shanghai at the Oriental Sports Center's indoor stadium from 16 to 31 July. There was a lot of hype surrounding the champion, Phelps, who was predicting that world records were going to fall in Shanghai. I always followed Phelps in the media, and it was interesting to note that he was saying that professional swimmers had to be in better shape and focus on the small things that would eventually make a big difference.

In the 200 m freestyle final, Phelps showed some weakness. Despite producing a strong performance, he was forced to accept the silver medal, as he was beaten by Ryan Lochte. That performance came on the back of a bronze medal for Phelps as a member of the 400 m freestyle relay. It was not often in his career that Phelps had entered a third event without a gold medal.

So, when Phelps stepped on to the starting blocks for his favourite event, the 200 m butterfly, the anticipation was at an all-time high. The world number one did not disappoint and won this event for the fifth time in his career. I managed a credible fifth-place finish, with 155.07 seconds. That performance managed to get my world rankings up, but I was still behind Michael Phelps, who won with a time of 153.3. But I was now closing in on Phelps – only about two seconds away from the world's best: I was getting faster.

In reality, however, those two seconds meant I was still a long way off him. At that point, Phelps hadn't lost in the 200 m butterfly for almost ten years. I continued to admire his performances, and it was still my ambition to stand on the same podium as my boyhood swimming hero at the Olympics.

In this race, it seemed as if Japan's Takeshi Matsuda, who had entered the competition with the fastest time in the world that year, could have dethroned Phelps and inflicted a second straight individual victory over him. At the 150 m mark, Phelps trailed Matsuda, but as he has done so often, Phelps floored it on the last lap to claim the gold. This time, he had to dig a bit deeper, though – but that's what champions do. Phelps said afterwards, 'The race felt good. I wanted to do what I usually do when

I'm in better shape. I wanted to step on it from the get-go. I saw the other swimmers at the 150 and I put my hips into it. I know there's a lot more I can do in that race.'

If there had been any doubts about Phelps's earlier performances in Shanghai, his triumph in the 200 m butterfly was proof that, no matter how off form he seemed to be, he was special. In the 100 m butterfly, which Phelps also won, I finished 13th; I finished 10th in the 4 x 100 m relay. At that stage, my breaststroke was getting worse, as the injury I was carrying hampered my movement through the stroke a lot.

At this point in the year, I was going through a lull, considering how well I had performed the previous year. So far, 2011 had brought nothing spectacular. I knew that I had to stay focused on my goal, however, which was the 2012 London Olympics, and continue to give it my all in training.

Things picked up. The FINA World Cup series, which included seven short-course meets in Dubai, Stockholm, Moscow, Bonn, Singapore, Beijing and Tokyo, took place over five-and-a-half weeks in October and November. In the Stockholm leg of the World Cup, I won one gold and three silver medals. My time for the gold medal was 1:54.33 in the 200 m backstroke, ahead of Brazil's Leonardo Fim (1:54.43) and Switzerland's Lukas Rauftlin (1:56.08).

My three silver medals came in the 200 m freestyle, 100 m butterfly and the 200 m IM. In the 200 m freestyle, I was beaten by Germany's Paul Biedermann (whose time was 1:43.44). I touched the wall in 1:43.80. The bronze medal went to Japan's Yuya Horihata (1:45.79).

In the 100 m butterfly, Tyler McGill claimed the top spot with a time of 51.04. I came second with 51.15 and Australia's Geoff Huegill was third with 51.36. I clocked a fast 1:54.93 for my third silver in the 200 m IM, but Daiya Sato from Japan beat me with 1:54.65 to claim the gold, and the bronze went to another Japanese swimmer, Hidemasa Sano (1:55.01).

I was thrilled to finish as overall winner and claim the grand prize of $100 000, which no one had expected me to win. With the lucrative cash incentives for performance, this World Series has now begun to attract a much more competitive field than it used to. It is a gruelling competition, as there are about six races a day, with the finals in the evenings. As part of my planning for London 2012, Graham wanted to test my mental strength at this World Cup. If I could handle this, then I could handle anything.

Together with the prize money offered for gold medals ($1 500), silver ($1 000) and bronze ($500), I earned a cool overall total of $145 500. In second place was Japan's Hidemasa Sano and third was Germany's Marco Koch. My overall medal haul for this series was 23 golds, ten silvers and two bronzes – 176 points in total. With these results, I moved into the number two South African position behind Cameron van der Burgh, who had won in 2008 and 2009.

6 Pre-Olympic preparation: Europe 2012

'I told my dad that I wanted to be the first to beat Michael Phelps. I would rather lose to the best than win by default.'

This was the year I would compete in my first senior Olympic Games. My training programme was going well: from early January to the beginning of March it was full-on, solid training. In fact, I was so committed that I was overtraining and doing more than Graham expected of me. I kept this from Graham and Dad's attention, though. I felt that, as this was the year of the Olympics, I had to give that bit more and prepare myself as best as possible.

I was working to improve my breaststroke, as this was my Achilles heel. At the end of 2011, I weighed 85 kg; in January 2012, the scales were showing 79 kg. The weight loss was due to the excessive training. I was too light – ideally, I needed to be around 83 kg. In March I ended up getting sick from overdoing the training. This foolishness was reflected in my performance at the national trials for the Olympics, held in Durban in April.

My mother, father and Jordan went ahead and booked their flights for London at the beginning of the year before I had even qualified. 'At least *we* are going to the London 2012 Olympics. We don't know about *you*,' Jordan teased.

The family support I received at the Olympic trials was outstanding. My father's side of the family is big – he is one of ten children. With all the relatives, there were more than 60 people supporting me.

In the 200 m butterfly, I won comfortably and made the FINA automatic qualifying standard, but I'll admit that my time of 1:56.17 was a bit slower than Graham and I had expected. This was the consequence of my fatigue, and the effect of wear and tear after my heavy schedules at the World Cup series and excessive training. People who knew me well could see the cracks in my performance. I guess they based their reservations on my quicker time in the semi-final of 1:55.30. In the final I didn't do particularly badly in any lap of the swim: it was just an overall slower performance.

As for the other qualifiers, in the 200 m IM, I was drawn against Darian Townsend, who I anticipated would be tough competition. I did not disappoint my fans, though, and won my third individual event with a time of 1:58.97. This was my fourth FINA Olympic qualifying time, with Darian posting his first qualifying time, finishing second in 1:59.34.

As the qualifiers went on, I could feel the effects of fatigue. My performance in the 100 m butterfly was quite poor, even though I won. My time of 52.45 was slower than I had achieved in other unrested meets. This was a direct result of the heavy training load I had imposed on myself. My coach suggested that I should consider dropping this event for the Olympics and just compete in the 200 m butterfly, the two IMs and a pair of relays (400 m medley and 800 m free). The idea was proposed because the 100 m butterfly was scheduled to come the day before the medley finals, and if I wanted to challenge for a medal in the medleys, missing the 100 m butterfly may have been a sensible option.

Some of my critics – other swimmers and provincial coaches – were saying that I needed to cut down on the events I competed in and adopt a less-is-more approach to my schedule at the 2012 Olympics. Their take was that I was only 20, and that I hadn't had enough experience to earn my stripes. This attitude reminds me of comments made about a certain David who went on to slay a giant.

Despite being run down (and despite the comments), I still managed to qualify for five races at the London 2012 Olympics – 200 m butterfly, 200 m IM, 400 m IM, 200 m freestyle and 100 m butterfly. Only Michael Phelps and Ryan Lochte had also achieved this feat. But it did take a lot out of me. It meant that, for each of these races, I would have to compete in three races (heat, semi and final), except for the 400 m IM, which had only the heat and the final. These five races were exactly the same events that Phelps had won in the 2008 Olympics. This was no coincidence: I wanted to race against him.

Qualifying for five races was an amazing accomplishment and a first for a South African swimmer. I didn't let this go to my head, though, as there was still a huge task that lay ahead of me, as Graham and I had reasoned.

When my dad saw the tough field of qualifiers whom I was going to be up against, he said that he hoped Phelps and Lochte would retire. I told him that, on the contrary, I wanted to be the first to beat Phelps. I would rather lose to the best than win by default. That's me: no excuses – period.

After having learnt from my mistake of overtraining, I reverted to the schedule that Graham and I had agreed to do. After the trials, I would swim 5–6 km a day, and then I progressed steadily to 10 km. At that stage, I had reached the hard grind around two months before the Games. Sticking to the programme, however, felt much better. I was very confident not only in the way I was swimming, but also in the way the whole team was swimming: we were performing really well around two months before the London Olympics. At this point, we started cutting down on the training load. I didn't want to make the same mistake again and burn myself out.

The hardest part for me was conditioning myself not physically but mentally to swim all those races. I was very proud of my achievement, but under no illusion that what lay ahead would be easy. You can't exactly take it easy in the heats or in the semi-finals if you want to reach the final: you are racing with the best in the world in each heat, so just to make the final was going to be a monumental effort.

The approach taken by the media was that I was expected to perform well. The sports press was quoting bookmakers who were giving me good odds to win a medal at least:

Chad le Clos will add to South Africa's medal tally at the 2012 London Olympics – if bookmakers are to be believed. Leading SA bookies, Ladbrokes, have quoted Le Clos as favourite for the bronze medal at 10/1 in Tuesday evening's men's 200 m butterfly final … Le Clos represents SA's last chance for a medal in the pool, after Cameron van der Burgh set a new world record in winning Sunday's men's 100 m breaststroke gold medal.

Graham tried his best to deflect the media attention and take the pressure off how I was expected to perform by encouraging me to take the angle that London 2012 would be a learning experience rather than an anticipated medal haul, and that the Rio 2016 Games should be my focus for gaining medals, and this was the reality proposed to the public at the time through the media: 'Le Clos has always maintained that he would be targeting the 2016 Rio de Janeiro Games as his pinnacle but he will, nevertheless, take a stab at it in the English capital.'

In an interview, Graham Joffe quoted Graham Hill as saying that '2016 was the focus for silverware', but then put the pressure on me by indicating that, based on my recent successes, I should be expecting some medals. My response was:

> Hopefully my main Olympics will be in 2016 – that is the goal that me and Graham have always had since I was a young boy. So ... these Olympics ... will be a bonus for me, I am going to go there fully prepared, of course, in the best shape of my life. Just to go there and enjoy it and enjoy the experience of competing against the best in the world.

And I was determined to go to London fully prepared and in great shape. There was no question of that. I wasn't planning to go there merely to enjoy the experience of competing against the best in the world. One of the special things about London 2012 was that I would be swimming in the same five events as Michael Phelps. That was very important for me, and it suddenly gave me a flashback to 2004, when I first saw Phelps blaze his way in the pool in the Athens Games. I always lived for the day that I would race against him at the Olympics – just to compete against him, one of the greatest Olympians of all time, was a great honour for me. I had made no secret of my desire to beat Phelps. Since the Commonwealth Games in 2010, Graham and I had been developing and improving our plan to beat Phelps. We were prepared to get there in small steps.

We left on 28 May for Europe to execute our final preparations for the London 2012 Olympics. It was two months before the Olympics and it meant that I was going to be away from home for 10 to 12 weeks. I went to my room and said out loud, 'The next time I come back to my room, I'm going to be an Olympic champion.'

It turned out to be a prophetic declaration.

Mare Nostrum

The South African team's participation in the 2012 Mare Nostrum – an event hosted by three Mediterranean countries – started off our 11-week swimming campaign away from home, culminating in the Olympics in the final two weeks. First, we stayed in the principality of Monaco for four days, where we worked on our tapering and final polishing. Then we travelled to Italy for our training camp. We flew to Rome and then bused to the Italian Adriatic coastal town of Pescara. I had to miss the Barcelona stage of the Mare Nostrum, as I had a post-nasal drip so I couldn't compete.

These were the hardest three weeks of training in my life: I worked on everything that I still needed to perfect. This involved focusing a lot on my breaststroke and butterfly. We were training in Mediterranean temperatures of around 37 °C and unbearable humidity. The hardest part was getting used to the heat, and Graham was like a sergeant major training us as if we were at war. Because of the heat, we would start training at 5:30 a.m. There was a lot of physical exercise every day, with no chance of having my usual recovery day. When Miles, my training partner, was doing recovery, I was doing breaststroke with Cameron, Julio and Marco Kock – really talented breaststrokers.

After Pescara, the team went back to Monaco for two weeks, where we were insulated from all the hype and buzz of the impending Olympics and this helped keep us away from the media spotlight, which can be a distraction. This helped me immensely from a psychological perspective.

In Monaco we were treated to a royal lunch at the palace of South Africa's Princess Charlene and Prince Albert II of Monaco. It was a black-tie formal affair and we all looked dapper in our penguin suits. Our hosts made the team a cake to wish us well. That evening, Prince Albert wished us good luck and mentioned that he had enjoyed hosting us.

I had first met Charlene when she was a member of Seagulls. In her day, she was an accomplished swimmer and represented South Africa. She won several national titles, including three gold medals and a silver medal at the 1999 All-Africa Games in Johannesburg. She was a member of the South African women's 4 x 100 m medley team at the 2000 Sydney Olympics. She retired from competitive swimming in 2007. She had her sights set on making a comeback in Beijing 2008, but injury prevented her from competing.

Graham, who had coached her, had been present when Prince Albert II had invited Charlene to dinner during the 2001 Mare Nostrum in Monaco. Graham jokes that little did he ever imagine that it would eventually lead to a royal marriage.

In 2013 I met Charlene again when we did a photo shoot for a women's magazine. She has always had a heart to help others. Her foundation (the Princess Charlene of Monaco Foundation) is focused on helping children. She hand-picks projects that are close to her heart and connected with

South Africa. Even though she is based in Monaco, she still visits South Africa to do what she describes as 'her bit'. Charlene is a remarkable woman who believes strongly that our actions make a difference. She desires to instil values that are important for the generations to come, and one that is close to her heart is to show boys how to respect women.

Charlene also supports the Get the Girls to Gold programme, which aims to help achieve at least two South African female medals in Rio 2016. This is a cause that I have also thrown my support behind. Charlene's foundation has sponsored an upgrade to the Seagulls club in Lahee Park, Durban. One of the major projects of her foundation is a learn-to-swim programme.

Graham also acknowledged how grateful we all were for her assistance during our stay in Monaco. It helped build our confidence and our team psychologist said that it was key to our success. Her moral support, the experience she had as an Olympian swimmer and her constant presence at the pool during our training calmed us and lifted our spirits.

To this day, my family and I remain close friends with Prince Albert and Princess Charlene.

At that stage of my preparation, my swimming schedule was 10 km a day, and on race days I was swimming 3 km before the race and another 2 km after. This training plan conditioned me very well and I knew that by the time of the Olympics I was going to be quicker.

It was great to have Shanky as part of our South African team to compete in London 2012. He qualified to participate in the 4 x 100 m medley relay event. His birthday fell while we were at our training camp in Pescara and I had to distract him while the rest of the gang set up the place for his party. I told him that we had booked him in for a physio appointment, but what I hadn't realised was that Shanky had already seen a Facebook post from his mother asking if we could arrange a cake for the celebrations.

In Pescara, after our training sessions, Shanky and I would enjoy chilling on the beach. We would swim out and relax in the warm Adriatic with the rest of the squad. In Monaco I had missed the opportunity of an invite to Charlene's holiday home because I had failed to get back in time for the team curfew. Shanky takes up this story:

Even with his 'sad face' on, Chad could not persuade Graham to let him come along. He had been caught on camera chatting up some girls. He was so engrossed in the conversation that he had lost all track of time.

Earlier, during our stay in Rome, we had gone on a bus tour of the ancient city. It was fascinating and I remember vividly how Chad was enthralled by the history of the place. Chad loves pasta. In Italy they serve the pasta dish first; the second course comes later. Chad pigged out so much on the pasta that he couldn't walk back to the room. His excuse was that it was too delicious.

Chad is paranoid that air conditioners make you sick. One time, he got out of the shower and insisted that I switch it off. He even took the remote, turned it off, then hid the remote. He cannot let an opportunity go by without doing something to annoy you. So, back at the hotel, while he was chilling in the jacuzzi, I took the shower head and sprayed him with cold water. Not to be outdone, he got out and what ensued was a water fight of great proportions.

Chad has kindly mentioned that I helped him study for his final exams, so it's good to know that he felt I was part of his 'support crew' that helped him get three As in matric in history, life orientation and maths – a great achievement under the circumstances.

In the second leg of the Mare Nostrum, held in Canet, in the south of France, in the 200 m butterfly I was in sizzling form, winning gold with a time of 1:55.46. That time ranked me seventh in the world for the year, though I had already swum a fifth-ranked time of 1:55.30. Kaio de Almeida of Brazil, who had won the first leg in Barcelona, finished second with a time of 1:56.10, while France's Jordan Coelho took third with 1:58.73. In the 200 m IM, I also blitzed the opposition and won in 2:01.14, winning the gold from Brazil's Henrique Rodrigues (2:02.37) and Canada's Tobias Oriwol (2:02.58).

After Canet, I won golds in Monaco in the 200 m IM, 200 m butterfly and 400 m IM. In the 200 m butterfly, I posted 1:55.77. Venezuela's Alexis Márquez Rivas finished second in 2:01.45, while India's Aaron Agnel D'Souza touched third in 2:02.30. Later in the meet, I picked up a second win in the men's 200 m IM with a time of 2:01.02. Justin James of Australia finished second (2:02.63) and Oriwol was third (2:03.63).

I followed these two gold medals with my third and fourth wins of the meet in the men's 100 m butterfly (52.43) and 400 m IM (4:21.39).

Going into the London Olympics, I felt that I was in the best shape of my life. I was confident that all the training and preparation were going to pay off, and I knew that after subjecting myself to the conditioning and sacrifices I had made, I would be disappointed if I didn't come away with at least one medal.

I had been training my whole life for this moment. Since I was 12, I had dreamt of this, and was relishing the opportunity to swim against my idol, Michael Phelps. Now that dream was about to become a reality.

7 The big one: Olympic Games, London 2012

'This is the last time you will ever get to race Michael Phelps in the 200 m butterfly. If you want to beat him, you have to beat him tonight.'

We arrived in London on 22 July – six days before the opening ceremony of the Olympics – and after our intensive preparation and training in the Mediterranean, the South African team was feeling relaxed and confident. I could sense immediately that the vibe was different from any other event I had previously competed in. From the moment we entered the Olympic Village, I was blown away by the special atmosphere there. I had raced in the World Championships, the World Cup, the Commonwealth Games – all major international events – but the Olympics were different. I think it's because you are among the best of the best in the world from all the sporting codes.

On our first day at the Olympic Village, Graham allowed us to have a look around and do everything we needed to do. Graham always arranged for Shanky and me to room together, as he saw that we had the same focus, and always had each other's best interests at heart. We knew when to train and when to relax. Shanky and I went to the area where they had set out the Playstation game Fifa. There were also Xbox games and pool tables available for the athletes to use.

As Shanky and I were playing imaginary soccer on screen, it was distinctly uncanny to look around and see 'real' members of the Brazilian soccer team, like Alexandre Pato, while we competed with their names on the video game. It was amazing to be able to walk around and spot world-famous athletes in the Village. I saw the Dream Team from the US and one of my boyhood soccer heroes, Ryan Giggs, whom I spotted in the dining hall – an unforgettable moment for me.

Day 1: 28 July

When the first rounds started, I was competing in the first race – the 400 m IM, which I consider a very difficult race. I went through the heats comfortably and was seeded second for the final, gaining lane 5 position. Ryan Lochte of the US was in lane 3, Kosuke Hagino from Japan in lane 4 and, as Phelps was slowest qualifying, he was drawn in lane 8. As I walked out before the 21 000-strong crowd, it felt like I was in Old Trafford for a big game. I was nervous for this final – I really wanted to win a medal.

I held the lead after the opening length of the butterfly leg, but faded in the middle of the race to finish fifth in 4:12.42. Lochte went on to win convincingly. Thiago Pereira was second and Hagino third. I did achieve a personal best, but fifth place was not enough for a medal and unacceptable for me. Others reassured me it was okay finishing fifth, but I didn't agree: I had wanted a medal.

As I assessed that race, I wasn't feeling nervous, but I was trying to make myself nervous. That morning I had thought, 'Wow, this is really the Olympics.' The crowd was huge and I think they played a big role in working on my nerves. With the 400 m IM done, I drew from that experience and was going to use it as a stepping stone towards future glory.

The results of the 400 m IM final:

Rank	Athlete	Country	Time
1	**Ryan Lochte**	USA	4:05.18
2	Thiago Pereira	BRA	4:08.86
3	Kosuke Hagino	JPN	4:08.94
4	**Michael Phelps**	USA	4:09.28
5	**Chad le Clos**	RSA	4:12.42
6	Yuya Horihata	JPN	4:13.30
7	Thomas Fraser-Holmes	AUS	4:13.49
8	Luca Marin	ITA	4:14.89

So day 1 of the Olympics started off with a lot of nerves for me. On day 2, I was disappointed that I had not won a medal. But that was all going to change soon.

Day 3: 30 July

The day of the semi-final of the 200 m butterfly. I qualified second fastest; Takeshi Matsuda was first; and Phelps, in lane 6, had the fourth-fastest qualifying time. I was between the two of them in lane 5.

The four fastest times from the semi-finals were as follows:

Rank	Athlete	Country	Time
1	Takeshi Matsuda	JPN	1:54.25
2	Chad le Clos	RSA	1:54.34
3	Yin Chen	CHN	1:54.43
4	Michael Phelps	USA	1:54.53

Day 4: 31 July – a day to remember forever

In the morning of this historic day, I swam in the 4 x 200 m relay heats and our team qualified for the final, which was scheduled after the final of the 200 m butterfly. I went back to my room in the Athletes' Village and took a short nap. When I awoke, it was around four in the afternoon. I felt relaxed and watched a movie.

Before a big race, I make special notes and that day was no different, as this was going to be the biggest race – the most important four pool laps – of my life. I sat down in front of my laptop and decided to pen my thoughts:

Whatever happens tonight, you lived your dream
And your family is proud of you
If it goes well, focus on other races
If not, then remember never to give up – you are a champ!

I then pressed the 'enter' button ten times and wrote 'Chad le Clos, Olympic Champion'.

I decided to find out what Graham was up to. In the Olympic Village, the male swimmers were allocated the upper floor, so Graham and I decided to go out on the roof for a walk. It was a beautiful day with the sun shining and a gentle wind blowing. I remember asking Graham if it was okay that I felt so calm and wasn't feeling nervous. Graham said he felt the same and that this was a good sign – we felt calm because we had done all the necessary preparation we could, so we were ready. We then went back to Graham's quarters and Skyped his family back home. Graham's wife was a bit concerned that we seemed so relaxed and were perhaps taking things too easy. 'Don't you have to swim the final of the 200 m butterfly soon? Are you okay?' she asked.

As I look back, I remember that everything about that day was like a dream. It felt as if something special was in the air and something amazing was going to happen. Graham had been listening to the same song before the big races: 'Picture' by Kid Rock. On the bus ride to the pool, about two hours before the race, he played it for me.

That 'unbelievable' 200 m butterfly final

We arrived at the pool at 5:50 p.m. I began my pre-race preparation and Graham went through our plan. With about an hour and a half to go, I started my stretching exercises. One hour before the race, I dived in and began my warm-up swim, which we set for 25 minutes – the plan was to get out 35 minutes before the race.

Those were very emotional moments and a lot of thoughts were rushing through my mind. With 20 minutes to go, as I walked through the tunnel into the first call room, I turned and asked Graham if he had any last words. 'I'm going to be like Chubbs,' he said.

'Chubbs' was the name he used for my dad. And then he kissed me on my forehead. He had seen Dad do this many times. This added a nice personal touch, an indication of how close we had become over the years we had been together. Our relationship was more than just coach and student – and that moment crystallised it. From the early days of swimming in the pool at his house to the biggest stage in the world – the Olympic Games. Getting to London 2012 had been a team achievement.

Before we parted, Graham turned to me and told me what I needed to do. I will never forget those words: 'This is the last time you will ever get to race Michael Phelps in the 200 m butterfly. If you want to beat him, you have to beat him tonight. This is your last chance.'

He was right, it was going to be Michael's last race at the 200 m butterfly, so this was the only chance I would have to beat him. It was going to be a David and Goliath battle, and I was up against the Goliath of swimming. I was also doing it for my beloved South Africa.

It was now time for me to report to the first call room, where all the swimmers have to present their caps, goggles and swimsuits to make sure that they are FINA approved. I had no problems and went through.

I had my iPod in my ears, my cap in my left pocket and my goggles around my neck. I always carry a charm with me, which Jordan has made a habit of giving to me. Usually, before big races, he gives me some sort of good-luck gift. I proceeded into the second call room, which is most intimidating. It is like a classroom with mirrors on both sides, so you are watched from every angle. Maybe it's done on purpose to test you and your nerve.

To see the lane arrangements with the names of the competitors seemed surreal: Michael Phelps in lane 6, Matsuda in lane 4 ... and there was my spot in lane 5. This was finally the dream come true: but it was now also real – I was going to be racing alongside Phelps in an Olympic final. As I went into that Olympic final, my best time that year had been 155.07. The previous year, in Europe, while training hard on the circuit, I had done 157 seconds. So with my best time of 155, I knew I could better that here at the Olympics by at least two seconds and therefore 153 was on the cards. But I also had to beat Phelps at his own game in the underwaters.

But before that race, nobody could have expected me to break the 153-second barrier. Only one person had been faster without a bodysuit: that was Phelps, when he did it in 152 seconds and set a new world record without wearing a bodysuit.

My friend Ryan Passmore had made me a music mix, which I had not listened to until then. I had it playing on my iPod as I entered the swimming pool arena. It was a combination of my school, Westville High, chanting 'We want Chad' and some pumped-up music in the background. The punchline was the voice of actor Will Smith talking to his son in the movie *Pursuit of Happyness*, where he tells him to always pursue and protect his dreams, regardless of what other people tell you.

Ryan's passion is music and being a DJ:

Chad heard one of my mixes and asked if I could make a mix of his own choice of music. He took this to the 2010 Commonwealth Games in Delhi. Since then, it has become a tradition for me to put together music mixes for him. Initially, I thought he wanted the music to listen to on the plane or in his hotel room. I didn't realise he was listening to it before his races, and I was pleased when I found this out.

For the Olympics I gave him the 'Chad le Clos Olympic mix'. I composed it as a motivational piece to help him step up to the next level. As he went to the 2012 London Olympics, many thought he would be just another swimmer. My biggest fear was that after he won the gold, he would forget us and get new famous friends. However, after returning from London, he asked me to come around for a game of Fifa and stay for some of his dad's famous curry. From that day, I knew that he hadn't changed and he is still the same Chad le Clos that I have grown to respect.

I'm not very good with words and when I came across this dialogue in the Will Smith movie, I felt it conveyed the message I wanted Chad to hear: that he should not listen to people telling him he couldn't achieve his dreams. So I put it together with some upbeat music and our school chanting his name during one of his race meets.

That music was still playing in my ears as I entered the arena. When Phelps appeared behind me, the spectators went bananas and I could hear their cheering even through the earphones. Undeterred, I went through my formality, which is to engage my 'trigger'. This is a switch for me to shut out everything. I put on my game face and focus completely on the race ahead. The procedure I go through involves touching the water, touching my swimming trunks to make them wet, and then touching my mouth and heart twice. For that race, I also had another special 'trigger' – one that was reserved exclusively for those Games and one that will never be used again in another. Being an avid follower of Phelps for some time, I had observed that he performs a pre-race ritual, in the form of a slap on his body. When I heard that familiar slap, it spurred me on even more – that was my special 'trigger' for these Games. I was ready, bring it on! We were called to our marks, the starter's signal sounded and we went off. The exact time was 7:52.10.

After we dived in, I realised I had had a good start, as I was ahead when I came up. I had to stick to the race plan and stay close to Phelps. After the first turn, Michael was ahead – which was what we had expected; I was second, with Matsuda third. I knew if I was still with him at the 100 m halfway mark, I would stand a great chance to beat him. At turn two, Phelps was still ahead, I was second and Velimir Stjepanovic was moving up into third place. The key was to stay all the way with Phelps and build from the third 50 m lap.

Easier said than done, as Michael was going hard out and what I was attempting to do over the last 50 was something not many had achieved. Come to think of it, I couldn't remember anyone beating Michael over the last 50 m of a 200 m butterfly final for a long time. In the third lap, Matsuda put in a great swim and was now second behind Michael, who split 1:21.93. Turning for home, even though I had dropped to third, I looked left and right and said to myself that I could get at least silver.

That moment was when I began to draw on all the training sessions. I dug in deep to begin to reel Michael in. In those last 50 m, everything went into slow motion. I remember turning in the last 50 – I just looked at Michael underwater and realised this was my hero. In disbelief, I began saying to myself, 'I'm actually catching Michael, wow I'm doing it!' That made me press even more and realise that my dream could now become a reality. 'Oh my gosh, you can beat him!' I thought.

Graham has a distinct whistle that all of us at Seagulls recognise. I could hear his whistle now. As I was coming through the last 25 m, I looked over to my right and saw Phelps; I saw how close I was to him. I was thinking how I was closing in on him with every stroke. I had the confidence that I could beat him: our plan was working. Going into the Olympics with the training regime Graham and I had worked on, I was very fit – probably the fittest butterfly swimmer there. The key was to use the bottom half of my legs and hips like a dolphin to gain more power and speed.

Having watched all of Michael's races, I knew how strong he finished. It may sound crazy, but I actually thought I *was* Michael at the last turn. When I turned and looked at him, that split second was another trigger point for me. I remember thinking to myself, and my coach's words, 'Keep it long and make sure you don't shorten up.'

The last 20 m felt like it took ages. The wall was coming up fast and I had to remind myself not to put my head down too early – as I usually go wild and do this. It came down to the flags and, as Graham and I had laboriously planned over and over again, I knew that this was the part where I had to execute the final aspect of our plan to perfection and make sure I touched the wall hard. I did exactly everything according to plan, knowing that Michael would glide into the wall. My final touch had to be perfectly timed so that I hit the wall at full speed.

Coming into the last three strokes, Michael may have thought he had already won, but I executed my final touch with perfection and finished at full speed, stretching for the wall. I think I still have a bump on that middle finger from hitting the wall so hard on the last stroke.

Initially, I genuinely thought I had come second. But as I looked up and saw my name in first place, I celebrated by screaming 'yes!', punching the water and throwing my hands up in the air.

So many thoughts were racing through my mind, but my first reaction was to look for my family in the crowd. I screamed, 'We won!' 'We' meant my country, my family and my coach. It really didn't feel like an individual victory: it was not just my efforts that allowed me to achieve victory. It reminded me of François Pienaar, when he lifted the 1995 Rugby World Cup at Ellis Park.

My father has always said to me to go out and live my dreams, to never give up on my dreams. Being an Olympic gold medallist is something that I'd dreamt about, but never thought would come true. Some doubted that it would happen in this Olympics. My father was there to witness it coming true, and I think the cleaners needed a mop because he couldn't stop crying. Images of him crying with the South African flag wrapped around him went viral. He was super proud of me and just knowing that I had him with me, as well as the rest of my family back home, was hugely motivating.

I could also see Graham, Leith Shankland and Darren Murray (another member of the South African team) jumping up and down next to the pool. The crowd was initially stunned into silence. They were probably shocked at me having beaten Phelps. All the swimmers got out of the pool and came to congratulate me. Even Michael shook my hand in the pool. I was trying to contain myself from crying, as my emotions were beginning to overwhelm me. I got out and could not care less that my goggles were the wrong way round; honestly I didn't know.

Beating the unbeatable – many had thought that would be impossible.

The results of the 200 m butterfly final:

Rank	Athlete	Country	Time
1	Chad le Clos	RSA	1:52.96
2	Michael Phelps	USA	1:53.01
3	Takeshi Matsuda	JPN	1:53.21
4	Dinko Jukić	AUT	1:54.35
5	Tyler Clary	USA	1:55.06
6	Velimir Stjepanovic	SRB	1:55.07
7	Paweł Korzeniowski	POL	1:55.08
8	Yin Chen	CHN	1:55.18

Later, Leith pointed out to Graham and me that this was a repeat of what had happened in the Dubai World Cup. There, I had come fifth in the 400 m IM and then, two days later, I had won the 200 m butterfly in lane 5. The same happened at London 2012: fifth in the 400 m IM, drawn in lane 5 for the 200 m butterfly final and the gold: it was destiny.

Says Leith:

When he won that gold, I was so happy that I ran up and down the pool in hysteria. I even picked up Darren and hugged Graham. Seeing Chad cry at the medals ceremony made me cry as well, as I knew how hard he had worked to achieve it – believe me when I say that it was no lucky touch.

The surprise for me was his result in the 100 m butterfly, where he took a whole second off his personal best. I guess the high from the 200 m gold spurred him on. I wish Chad everything of the best for his future.

After the race, there were about 45 minutes to an hour before the relay, so I had to calm down. When I walked through the tunnel, all the media wanted to talk to me. I declined, as I had another race to prepare for. I ran to join my teammates, who were leaping into the air. Graham's first words to me were: 'Chad, well done. Now you need to calm down, as you have the relay coming up.'

I also had to go to the medal ceremony call room. This was the first time I had seen Michael since the race. Seeing him occupying the number-two position somehow didn't look right, and then it hit me even harder. I looked at Takeshi, at third, and I was speechless: that was my chair – first place, Chad le Clos. Michael came over and said to me, 'Hey, man, great job, great race.' I didn't quite know how he was going to react, as this result was not meant to happen. It was not the ending or the script that Team Phelps had wanted. I was feeling very emotional. I had always looked up to him and it was really hard for me to hear Michael say that. I was beginning to choke up. But I couldn't possibly cry in front of Phelps, so I had to disguise it by pretending there was something in my eye. Michael asked if I was all right. I went to the tap, splashed some water over my face to compose myself and walked out for the medal ceremony.

Seeing Sam Ramsamy of the IOC at the medal ceremony suddenly transported me back to the time he had told me that he was going to pick the race I was going to win and would be there to hand me the gold medal. He had said this months before the race. It was an extra blessing to have this South African icon hand me my first Olympic gold medal. Before my name was announced, I was biting my lip and trying very hard not to cry. But as Sam put the medal around my neck, I was already crying and had to wipe my face for the national anthem. I just couldn't believe it; I couldn't have imagined I'd be here having beaten Phelps. I had always dreamt of emulating Phelps since he won six gold medals at the 2004 Athens Games when I was just 12. He had always been an inspiration to me and a role model. Therefore, this race meant more to me than an Olympic final. I just wanted to try to beat him and when it actually happened, I couldn't really believe it because it was like this dream come true.

I was so caught up in my emotions that Michael had to remind me, 'Hey, man, you got to hold up your medal!' He was just great – he spoke to me throughout the ceremony, helping me out with the formalities. I was encouraged by what Michael said to the media:

> It is going to be fun to watch Chad and see what he does over the next four years. It has really been fun to race with him … and sort of get to know him … I am probably eight years older than him. Chad is a kid and he is going to be up here and it shows that anything that you want to achieve – if you put your mind to it – and you work hard, you can achieve it … He and his coach have worked together to be able to get where he is.
>
> Chad was there at the right place at the right time and he got his hand on the wall first. He is a very good competitor, a very hard-working kid, a very hungry kid.

After the medal ceremony, I went straight to the call room for the relay. We went off third with Townsend leading the team. After my gold medal, I was all pumped up. The relay went by fast. I was still probably trying to get over having beaten Phelps. I got a personal best in the relay, which showed I was still focused and I didn't want to let the team down. We finished seventh; Michael's US team won.

Had Michael won the 200 m butterfly, he would have been the first person to win it three times in a row at the Olympics. I denied him that record. Phelps later tweeted: 'Can't express enough about the amazing swim Le Clos had tonight in the 200fly!! Well done kid!!'

After the Olympics, there was a dinner arranged with my family and we invited Michael. They were all hugely impressed by him. He is still my hero – but now I can also say he is a friend. After his retirement, he told me he would like to visit South Africa and do a shark-cage dive. I am looking forward to that.

Dad's memorable interview on the BBC went viral that night and #chads-dad was trending on Twitter.

When I got back to the Olympic Village, it was late – around two in the morning – but Shanky and Darren were waiting for me to celebrate. Nothing too serious, as I was racing later that morning in the 200 m IM heats. It was hard to sleep that night. And, yes, I did sleep with the gold medal around my neck.

I followed my fans on Facebook and Twitter. It was the first time I had logged in for over a month, as I don't do that during competitions. Before the Olympics, I had had a thousand followers, but by that night there were 25 000 and the number was growing through the night.

The next day, 1 August, was a tough morning of competition, because I hadn't had sufficient sleep, but I still made the semi-finals and then went on to make the finals, qualifying seventh. To be realistic, I did not have much of a chance at winning the 200 m IM, so Graham decided to pull me out of the event. He advised me that it was better that I scratched, as the final was scheduled for 2 August, the same day as the semi-final of the 100 m butterfly, in which I stood a better chance of medalling. I wasn't too happy, as I was not the type of person to scratch.

We debated it, but I finally decided to go along with Graham's advice. This was not well received by the IOC, who did not like our decision. Their reasoning was that for the 200 m IM final the field was Phelps, Ryan Lochte, Thiago Pereira, László Cseh, Kosuke Hagino and me, so it would have been the most decorated final. Phelps won, Lochte was second and Cseh third; Pereira finished fourth. I was really happy that Michael won and got the hat-trick – Athens, Beijing and London.

On 2 August the 100 m butterfly heats and the semi-final (at night) were held. I was shouting for Phelps to win when he swam in his 100 m butterfly semi-final, then I realised that I was going to meet him again in the final. He qualified with the fastest time; I was second fastest, which meant that we would be lining up alongside each other for the final – dubbed the 'rematch' – the next day.

100 m butterfly final: the 'rematch'

On the morning of the 100 m butterfly, I also had the 4 x 100 m medley relay, where I was swimming the butterfly leg. This was the seventh day of the Games and there was even more pressure on me now. I was disappointed because I had expected to make the relay final and I didn't. Six hours after the relay was the rematch, so I went back to my room and slept for about two hours and followed pretty much the same preparation routine as for my 200 m butterfly.

It was Phelps's last individual race and there was therefore more pressure on him than on me to win, as I had nothing to lose. I had reached five finals – a great achievement for my first Olympics appearance. But I was still looking for a medal. The atmosphere in the call room was reminiscent of the 200 m final: there was a great sense of expectancy weighing on me once again. I guess whenever Phelps competes, there will always be an aura of anticipation and excitement because of the sort of champion he is. I was confident that I could win, but knew that Phelps was even more motivated. There was even more rivalry in this race.

I didn't get the start I wanted, and at the wall Michael touched seventh and I was eighth. We turned almost simultaneously. In lane 6 was Čavić, who had finished second in the Beijing Olympics and who had almost stopped Phelps then. He was leading at the turn with a split of 23.36; Deibler from Germany was second and Czerniak third.

But Čavić faded as Michael hit the gas in the last 20 m and achieved another trademark victory, earning his 17th Olympic gold medal. I tied for silver with Yevgeny. My time of 51.44 seconds was 0.23 seconds behind Phelps. I was pleased with the silver but disappointed about not getting the gold. And that was my London 2012 over.

After the race, Phelps admitted on TV how important the gold had been in this, his last individual race:

> I wanted to win. I went slower than I did last night, but a win is a win, I can't complain. If I wanted to swim faster, then I should have prepared better. Looking back at this Olympics, everything that I did prior to this is my decision. I am happy and … I've been having fun this whole time.

After that race, when I look back, I was disappointed about my performance, and there were a few things I would have liked to have done differently. In the end, Phelps was the better athlete. As I become a more mature swimmer, I won't make those mistakes again. I did mention immediately after the race on TV that I was proud of Michael's three gold medals in the 100 m butterfly in three consecutive Olympics. Emotionally overcome by my victory, I was almost in tears in that interview, but it was Yevgeny Korotyshkin who was really emotional and overwhelmed by his joint silver medal.

The results of the 100 m butterfly final:

Rank	Athlete	Country	Time
1	Michael Phelps	USA	51.21
2	Chad le Clos	RSA	51.44
2	Yevgeny Korotyshkin	RUS	51.44
4	Milorad Čavić	SRB	51.81
4	Steffen Deibler	GER	51.81
6	Joeri Verlinden	NED	51.82
7	Tyler McGill	USA	51.88
8	Konrad Czerniak	POL	52.05

As I reflected on my two medals back in the Olympic Village, I felt grateful to my teammates, who had been so supportive. Cameron van der Burgh said some really nice stuff to the media about me: 'We're all very proud and are going to need new voices after the past four days. I was more nervous watching it than my own race. It gave me some perspective of what I did the other night watching someone else do it. That boy works harder than anyone else. He deserves it.'

I was motivated by Van der Burgh's success and by his win in the 100 m breaststroke, and hoped that it would spur the rest of the South African team on for the rest of the Games. Hopefully, our gold medal performances will be the start of a new golden era for South African swimming. We had a lot of support back home. I think we had a fantastic group of swimmers at the 2012 Olympics, and for 2016 it's looking very positive because there are a number of talented swimmers who can make it. I think the future is bright for South African swimming.

In an interview shortly after London 2012, Michael Phelps admitted that he didn't like losing and the hardest loss for him was when I beat him in the 200 m butterfly, and handed him his third defeat in the last ten years. Michael acknowledged that I was better prepared and conceded that that was why I touched first.

Much has been written about my victory over Phelps. As I look back, I want people to understand three major things about my gold medal victory at London 2012. Firstly, never give up. Despite what negative things people might say, you can achieve your dreams. I was facing my idol and one of the greatest Olympians of all time, but I stayed focused on my goal and came out on top in spite of the odds. Be encouraged that anything can be achieved regardless of the obstacles that you are up against.

Secondly, finish strong. I have often heard it say that it's not so much how you start, but how you finish. Many have said that Phelps made a mistake by gliding home in the final, but the main point is that I was relentless all the way and turned it on at the finish, all the way to the end. I had practised and trained hard to do that in those last few metres. So, when chasing a goal, push yourself all the way to the end and you will be surprised at the result you get. Don't settle for less than giving your best. This is what my dad taught me from when I was young. I don't ever want to be average. After all, average is the best of the worst and the worst of the best. Our limitations in life are mostly in our head and not physical – no matter how hard you try, you can go further and work harder. My final seconds of that race prove this theory.

Finally, set yourself goals and have a vision. Having seen Phelps win in 2004, I set myself the goal to race against him one day in the Olympics and beat him. From setting that goal to accomplishing it took eight years and a lot of hard work. How did I do it? I held on to my vision and didn't let anything stop me from pursuing it. It is said that you only start to see obstacles when you take your eyes off your goals.

I want to acknowledge the great champion that Phelps is and how much he has contributed to swimming worldwide. He has led the way and I hope to be able to follow his example, as he has inspired so many. My aim is to take swimming to greater heights and I know that I can make a difference.

8 Proudly South African

'Sport has the power to change the world.'
– Nelson Mandela

We had been back in South Africa for a couple of days after the London Olympics. Dad and I decided to do a quick grocery shop. Quick, however, it didn't turn out to be: we were mobbed by shoppers at the supermarket. Everyone, it seems, wanted a piece of both of us – Dad was an immediate hit back home as well, and now he had to field calls from the media, cover as my personal assistant, as well as act as my bodyguard when we went shopping.

Being back home after all the attention at the Olympics gave me some time to unwind. People ask me what I do to relax and I explain that swimming takes up so much of my time that I don't get to do a lot of things that other guys my age enjoy. To relax, I enjoy being outdoors, going to the beach, catching a few waves at the weekend, which is definitely one of my favourite pastimes. I'm also a huge Playstation/Fifa fan. Usually on Thursdays, our recovery day, a group of friends comes over to play three-a-side.

Some argue that, because of the international nature of my swimming career, it's premature for me to claim that I intend to remain in South Africa. But I love my country and I am 'proudly South African'. There is a lot to be done for swimming in South Africa: it's a sport that plays second fiddle to the much more popular and commercial sports like rugby, cricket and soccer. I want to help change this status of swimming in my country, so relocating overseas would not be right.

There are currently only about 3 000 swimmers registered with swimming clubs affiliated with Swimming South Africa, but I know that South Africa has a lot more talented young swimmers who just need motivation. I can help provide that motivation to inspire young swimmers and help to make South Africa a swimming superpower. I realise that it is challenging with a sport like swimming, in South Africa, to gain local sponsors, as it is very much the poor relation of the big three. So most of our sponsorship comes from international organisations. We are obviously delighted to have these sponsors, but, as swimmers and Olympic athletes, we also need corporate South Africa to become more involved in swimming.

What does it mean to me to be South African?

As a child, I grew up watching the Springboks and Bafana Bafana perform – teams that have brought national pride to our country. My aim is to do the same with swimming. I know that sport can play a huge role in bringing a nation together, as former president Mandela showed during the 1995 Rugby World Cup, when he wore the Springbok's shirt in a gesture that so clearly showed how a once racially divided nation could be united in sport. Sport has that special ability to bring everyone together.

Ask any kid after a rugby, soccer or cricket international who they would want to be like when they grow up and they will say Bismarck du Plessis, Patrick Lambie, Lawrence Siphiwe Tshabalala or AB de Villiers. It's as if South Africans feel that they are part of their national sides, that they are actually playing for them. This is something I've always felt.

The first time I watched a live rugby game was in 2007. It was a Tri-Nations Test between South Africa and the mighty All Blacks. We lost that game, which was a close encounter, but it was the first time I had heard the national anthem being sung by so many thousands at a stadium. It was such an overwhelming experience that I cried. In a Test match there is more at stake than the trophy: it's a whole nation's pride, the national badge. I have always believed that sport has the capacity to bring a nation together, and that's important. It is one of the reasons why I love South Africa.

The country has experienced the huge political challenge of its transition to democracy. And there may well be good professional reasons why I should leave South Africa and base myself in the US – but the fact is, I don't want to. It would not be the same; it's not who I am. Yes, I would make my millions, but it's not the same as living where you come from. You will no doubt have seen movies made by people who have made their fame and fortune and who then produce a movie about where they come from. US actor and producer Mark Wahlberg is one example with his film *Entourage*, where he shared his past experiences. In the international arena of swimming, South Africa may not be at the same level as America, but I know we can get there.

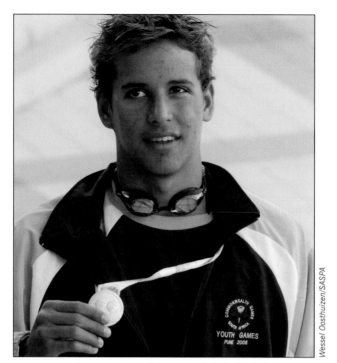

Wessel Oosthuizen/SASPA

With my gold medal at the Commonwealth Youth Games in India on 16 October 2008. The SA team provided me with the opportunity to compete after another swimmer meant to participate in the event was injured – I was only 16. I'm glad I didn't let them down. I also proved myself as a sportsman to keep an eye on.

Ian Walton

Riaan Schoeman and me at the 2010 Commonwealth Games' medal ceremony in India on 7 October 2010.

Here I am competing against my sporting idol, and the world's best swimmer, Michael Phelps, in the 200 m butterfly final at the London Olympic Games, 31 July 2012. It took a lot of hard work, and not chance, for me to get to this point - and to get the gold medal at the end of all of it.

For just a moment I thought I had won the silver. Then I heard my name being called as the winner of the 200 m butterfly. I had won an Olympic gold medal and beaten my idol, Michael Phelps, in the competition he was most famous for. The joy and pride I felt are indescribable.

Fist pumps all around as we celebrate that 'unbelievable' victory. My father garnered worldwide fame for his emotional response to my win. This win wasn't just for me, but also for my family, my friends and my country.

Me and Princess Charlene, a former Seagull, at the Pinetown swimming pool where we both used to train, Durban, August 2012. Charlene is passionate about her charitable endeavours in South Africa. One of her goals is to upgrade the swimming facility in Pinetown to attract a greater number of young swimmers. She is determined to produce more SA swimming talent.

Me and fellow Olympic medal winners, Cameron van der Burgh, Bridgitte Hartley, Caster Semenya, Matthew Brittain, Sizwe Ndlovu, John Smith and James Thompson during the South African Olympic team arrival and press conference at OR Tambo International Airport on August 14, 2012 in Johannesburg.

Duif du Toit / Gallo Images

Taking a pic with Cameron and a few fans at OR Tambo International after arriving from the London Olympics, August 2012. Cameron is a great competitor and one of South Africa's best swimming talents.

Gallo Images/Foto24/Felix Dlangamandla

A fan holding up a poster asking me to be her date to her matric farewell on August 9, 2012 in Johannesburg. Hundreds of people gathered at OR Tambo to welcome me and the rest of SA's London Olympic athletes home, which was very touching. I am exceedingly grateful to all of my fans for their support and I try to show this gratitude as much as I can through social media, meeting fans and this book!

Wessel Oosthuizen/SASPA

Me and Graham at a press conference at Team SA's media centre in Kensington, UK in August 2012.

Lefty Shivambu/Gallo Images

I was so proud to be named Sports Star of the Year at the SA Sports Awards in 2012.

I was appointed an Omega brand ambassador in 2011. This is me signing the Omega wall-of-fame in 2012.

Arena is one of the leading watersports brands in the world. They've been a sponsor of mine since 2010 and I'm very grateful for all of their support.

Future Life is a big part of my nutritional plan. It provides me with the necessary fuel to help sustain my diet which supports a hectic training regimen.

Ezemvelo KwaZulu-Natal: Jabulani Ngubane, myself, Dr Bandile Mkhize (CEO), and my dad. I am a proud ambassador for Ezemvelo KZN Wildlife's rhino initiative. The organisation has done much for rhino conservation efforts. I am determined to help fight this attack on Africa's wildlife and this is a cause I am passionate about.

Sports Star of the Year Award

Receiving the South African Sports Star of the Year Award for 2012 was a momentous thing for me. The fact that I had been voted by the people of South Africa made it all the more special: it meant I was the 'people's champion'. I hope youngsters will say, 'I want to swim like Chad le Clos' and I want people to see that they can be like me. To win this top accolade when there were other great contenders, like cricketers Hashim Amla and Vernon Philander, athlete Caster Semenya and Bafana Bafana's Siyabonga Nomvethe, was really humbling and such an honour for me.

The R1 million prize money and the brand-new BMW were also nice trophies to walk away with. I gave my mother the car; and the cash – well, let's just say it's wisely invested.

Order of Ikhamanga

The Chancellor of the National Orders, Dr Cassius Lubisi, announced that I was to be awarded National Orders at an investiture ceremony to be held on Freedom Day, 27 April 2013, with that year's ceremony being held under the theme of 'mobilising society towards consolidating our democracy and freedom'. President Jacob Zuma would bestow the awards. I was ecstatic, as the National Orders are the highest awards that a country, through its president, confers on its citizens and eminent foreign nationals who have contributed towards the advancement of democracy and who have made a significant impact on improving the lives of South Africans. The National Orders also recognise the contributions made by individuals to a non-racial, non-sexist, democratic and prosperous South Africa, as envisaged in the Constitution. I received the Order of Ikhamanga in Silver for my 'excellent achievements on the international swimming stage, especially at the London Olympics in 2012, thus placing South Africa in high standing globally in the field of aquatic sports'.

Ironically, due to my swimming commitments, I could not make the event, so I sent my regards and thanks to the president. This was a special 21st birthday present for me and a huge honour. The last time it was awarded was 12 years ago. It's an honour I liken to a British person receiving an OBE. But it's also just good to be recognised for what you've done. Every athlete, every person, likes to be acknowledged for and feel proud of their achievements. You mustn't be vain but you should be able to feel proud of what you've done. I'm very proud of what I've achieved. Sometimes I think about how I've done something that no one else has done: I am the only person to have beaten Michael Phelps in a butterfly final.

In the context of great achievements, it can be the small things, the details, that make the big difference – like putting my head down to create a streamlined profile at the finish of a race. You wouldn't be reading this book today if I hadn't done that: I would have won the silver and no one would really have cared. That extra turn to create a fluid movement or that extra fly kick underwater can make the biggest difference in a race.

Laureus World Sports Awards

It was such an honour for me and my dad to be invited to the prestigious Laureus World Awards in 2013 in Rio, Brazil. It was an incredible experience to find ourselves among past and current international sports stars.

The Laureus Sport for Good Foundation's goal is to help young people overcome the limitations imposed by challenging social issues, including poverty, homelessness, conflict, violence, drug abuse, discrimination and AIDS. To fulfil this, the Laureus Foundation supports and assists a worldwide programme of sports-related community projects that have been working for over ten years to educate children, protect the vulnerable from illness and even bring people from divided communities together in friendship.

The foundation's mission is to use the power of sport as a tool for social change. This mission was inspired by the words of the foundation's former patron, Nelson Mandela, who, at the first Laureus World Sports Awards in Monaco in 2000, said: 'Sport has the power to change the world. It has the power to inspire. It has the power to unite people in a way that little else does. It speaks to youth in a language they understand. Sport can create hope where once there was only despair.'

On the plane trip we had a great time with Springbok legend, Morné du Plessis. What a gentleman! We stayed at the Copacabana Hotel, one of the best hotels in the world, where we met tennis legend Björn Borg. He came up to my dad while I was training in the pool. He said that he and his wife had been enjoying watching the Olympic champ swim. Brian

Lara, the West Indian cricket icon, was also at our hotel. Lara was very friendly, as was former All Black great, Sean Fitzpatrick. We all got to know one another and they made us feel really welcome.

After the awards, I was feeling unwell, which caused me to hold up the shuttle bus that was taking us back to the hotel. Someone got impatient and insisted that the bus shouldn't have to wait. My dad was not happy and suggested that, if that were the case, then we would catch a taxi. At that point, Sean Fitzpatrick intervened with the impatient passenger: 'Excuse me, Sir. I am part of the Laureus organisation and as this is a bus for the Laureus guests, it's not moving until we wait for the gold medallist, Chad le Clos.' That completely changed the attitude of that man; after he had found out that I was a gold medallist, he spoke with us for an hour and a half.

At the event we also met Sir Bobby Charlton and Michael Johnson, the 200 and 400 m sprinter. When my dad asked him for a photograph, he treated us like we were royalty. He said to Dad, 'I want a photo with you, as you're an inspiration to how fathers should be around the world.' Even Germany's soccer legend Franz Beckenbauer socialised with us and I remember him calling my father Bertie.

It was amazing how these sports icons were so down to earth and humble. There were no complexes or boundaries – they didn't regard themselves as big shots. Dad and I felt like kids in a candy store.

The Laureus is a huge event and one of the most enjoyable I've been to. What an honour to be invited by the Laureus committee. Being in the company of legends and seeing how gracious they were towards us was inspiring. Some of them were my heroes when I was growing up and, now, here they were talking to me! That is something I will never forget and a very humbling experience. I asked Ed Moses for a photo while he was eating. He said he would pose for me after he had finished his meal – 'I'm sorry, man, just give me two minutes. I'll finish eating with my wife, and I'll come get you.' He said no, but he said it in a nice way, which is different to just saying no.

The highlight at the Laureus Awards was when Morgan Freeman, the master of ceremonies, asked, 'Where is Chad le Clos? Chad le Clos – is he here?' I put my hand up and he said, 'Son, just sit down: your dad is more famous than you and he is going to be signing autographs later. You have to go to bed because you got to swim in the morning.' I felt so impressed that they mentioned me and my dad at the event.

The Laureus Sport for Good Foundation is about giving something back to people. It is an organisation that I hope to be involved with one day. I want to be in a position someday when I can give something back. Sport has given so much to me and my family – and I don't mean just financially. It has given me so much in my life that I will never forget. I know that it has been hard work, and at times there are sacrifices I have had to make and injuries that I have sustained, but at the end of the day my sport has given me special memories and experiences.

My 21st birthday

This was a big night for me, as I had not had a party for a long time. We had taken some time off and were holidaying in Mozambique. Mum, Dad, Jordan and my sister, Bianca, were with me. Bianca organised everything. As a 21st birthday present, I was given a unique ring to mark the occasion. My parents paid a hefty R50 000 for it. It features the five interlocking rings of the Olympic Games symbol and is made of 18-carat yellow and white gold and set with 101 diamonds – 100 for show and one for good luck. Not a bad present to receive on your 21st!

Dad presented it to me after our holiday during lunch at the Ile Maurice Restaurant in Umhlanga. The owners, Jean Mauvis and Christian Lenferna, laid on a Mauritian feast to take us back to our family roots. Dad, who commissioned the ring, knew that I had wanted an Olympic ring for some time and decided to plan it for my 21st, which was perfect timing. Dad's take on it is that your 21st is when you get something special. 'Chad's reaction was unbelievable when he saw the ring. It really surpassed his expectations,' he says.

The ring was a 'three-way' gift to me. The design idea involved my dad, my cousin, Andrey Riethoven, a Durban diamond setter, and goldsmith/ designer David Bachelor. 'The project took about a month to complete. Although a lot of time and effort went into making this ring, I enjoyed every moment because of my relationship with Chad,' Andrey says.

We also held a party in Johannesburg on 26 April and another one the following day for my family and close friends – there were about 300 of them (I have a big family!). It was held at The Czar, in Durban, until 10:30 p.m., after which we opened up the party to the public.

My heroes

One of my heroes outside of swimming is the 'people's champion' Muhammad Ali. I recall Ali saying he was ready to fight his then opponent George Foreman anywhere, even in a phone booth. I respected what Ali stood for, even though he came across as arrogant and outspoken. He was famous for his 'I am the greatest' rants. He made the sport fun and he was exciting to watch. His poems and rhymes added a lot. Ali was not afraid to stand up for what he believed in. This reminds me of Nelson Mandela, for what he did for our country; and people like Sam Ramsamy, who had a part in the unification of sports in South Africa. Sam's actions helped make it possible for me to be at the Olympics. And Sam, and so many others, made a lot of personal sacrifices to stand up against injustice. I like people that stand up for justice and for worthy causes. Someone said if you don't stand up for something, you will fall for anything.

Michael Phelps, as I have mentioned, has always been a hero of mine, but closer to home there is South African swimmer Terence Parkin. I used to observe Terence training at Seagulls. He was the captain of the club and trained the hardest of anyone I had seen. He was so good at what he did, despite his disability, and I looked up to him. I admire people who are, or have been, the best at what they do. That's why I like Roger Federer and Rafael Nadal. You cannot win a gold medal at the Olympics by fluke, or take a grand slam without sacrifice and hard work. Terence was always really nice to me, happy to talk with us about anything and keen to help me when I was younger. He would motivate me to train hard. He wasn't a man of many words, but he possesses honour and integrity. We had five or six Olympians in our squad but he was 'killing' them all in every stroke. I admire him not for his silver medal at the Sydney 2000 Olympics, but more because he was a great guy and always approachable.

The standout point about Terence was that he never allowed his deafness to be an excuse or to hold him back. I don't think I would be as happy if I had such a disability. Terence never got upset and always kept his composure.

When your hero, or someone you look up to, talks to you or asks how you are, that's good enough. It's not about what they say to you, but more about the fact they have taken the time to engage with you. As an example, I had met Bismarck du Plessis for the first time in 2010. Later, when I was at Dubai Airport, he remembered who I was and came over to talk to me. He didn't have to do that, and I didn't even think he'd remember me. That was so special and I immediately called my dad to tell him what had happened. That is the sort of attitude that has always motivated me. Conversely, I can be very judgemental about famous sports-people when they are disrespectful, especially when it's shown to fellow players and coaches. I didn't like it when Carlos Tévez was disrespectful to his manager, Mancini, at Manchester City. The media grabbed that story and it did not set a good example to see how Tévez refused to play when his manager told him to get on to the field.

My causes

I have faced many challenges in my swimming career and each hurdle has required my utmost to dig deep for resources I did not know I had. Although I have scaled the heights in swimming, I also have other goals. I hope to make a difference through various worthy causes outside of swimming that are close to my heart. It is time for young leaders to show their mettle and stand up for a cause. I lay down the challenge to all to do what you can to make the world a better place.

My first cause is cancer. As mentioned earlier, I am a brand ambassador for CANSA. Through Mum's fight with breast cancer, she really inspired me and my whole family. She was cleared by the medical team but still has to take medication. I swam in one of the World Cup legs in Stockholm with a pink cap and coloured my swimming trunks pink, firstly in support of my mum and, secondly, to raise awareness of cancer by supporting the brave people who are fighting this dreadful disease.

I have always had a great passion for animals, as you would have read earlier about my affection for the cows on the milk cartons. Rhino poaching appals me and I want to help stop this decimation of the species. I want the youth of Africa and the world to stand up against this attack on one of God's creatures that we are entrusted to protect as a legacy for the next generations. I am pleased to be Ezemvelo Kwa-Zulu Natal Wildlife's rhino ambassador. This organisation has a proven conservation record in South Africa. At a function I heard about how the then Natal Parks Board had managed to bring the white rhino back from the brink of extinction in the 1960s by capturing and relocating the animals throughout southern Africa and overseas. This is an onslaught on Africa and I call on all Africans of all ages to deal with this challenge.

My sponsors

I am grateful to my sponsor Arena, one of the leading water-wear sports brands worldwide. They signed me in October 2010, the week before the Commonwealth Games in Delhi, and it meant a lot to be part of the same team as Aaron Peirsol, Alain Bernard, Cameron van der Burgh and Roland Schoeman. I think Arena became interested after taking note of my performances up to that time, notably on my 18th birthday at the South African Nationals, when I swam the world's fourth-fastest 200 m butterfly of the year (1:56.86), and then my gold at the inaugural Youth Olympics. Arena approached me and we agreed to a two-year deal running to 2012.

My victory in the IM in the Singapore Youth Olympics was so emphatic that it catapulted me into the top 25 in the world, and prompted The Swimmers' Circle blog to post: 'Times like Le Clos' give some serious legit-imacy to the event, and assuages fears from several federations (notably the British) that the level of competition wasn't worth the time and the money of sending a squad.'

Giuseppe Musciacchio, Arena's marketing director, said:

We are delighted to welcome Chad le Clos to our Elite Team. Over the past two years, Chad has shown what a prodigious talent he is, and his rise as a 17-year-old through to the ranks of the world's best senior swimmers has been nothing short of phenomenal. His gold and bronze in the 400 and 200 IM in Berlin showed what he is capable of, and he followed this up in 2010 with one of the year's best 200 m butterfly swims. He is clearly destined for greater things, not only in the medley and butterfly events, but also potentially in others, as his progress and results in both freestyle and breaststroke confirm. As the fourth South African member of our Elite Team, he demonstrates the strength of the sport in that country, and we expect him to produce more impressive results for himself and for Arena, both in and out of the pool.

Signing with Arena was the start of my professional career. I had always competed in Arena gear, and now to have a contractual relationship with the organisation was very exciting for a young guy like me. It really gave me a big morale boost.

My first interaction with Future Life was about a year before the London 2012 Olympics. I already enjoyed Future Life products as part of my diet and nutrition plan, then my agent advised me that he would make enquiries with the company to see if they would consider sponsoring me. Competing at the top level requires that I fuel up properly and Future Life was doing the job for me very well – I could feel the difference.

It was arranged for Dad and me to meet Future Life's CEO, Paul Saad. This is what Saad had to say about that meeting:

> In my first meeting with Chad, I observed that he was a humble and down-to-earth person. With him 'what you saw was what you got'. At the time, with regard to sponsorship, what he was asking for was not a lot. We dropped off more products with him with the message that we must have further discussions. The trouble I then faced was convincing the rest of our team that Chad was 'our man'. This turned out to be harder than I had envisaged – the rest of the team did not want to put sponsorship behind swimming, but rather allocate resources to sports that are actively supported in South Africa, like soccer, rugby and cricket.

Saad told me that when the London 2012 Olympics came around, he was very keen to follow my progress and remembers telling his wife that I was champion material and would do well there. He watched the final of the Olympics 200 m butterfly on TV, and was cheering me on as I won. Paul Saad was a great athlete in his school days and achieved national honours. I guess that's why he is so passionate about sports and understands some of the demands our bodies place on us. Athletics, like swimming, requires discipline and commitment. After my Olympic gold medal, he was quite emotional. Afterwards, he said: 'I had a hollow, sinking feeling that we were unwise in not having signed Chad. I was so happy for him on the one hand, but at the same time disappointed that we had let him go.'

So when I got back from London 2012, I received a call from him asking to meet. Then we signed the sponsorship deal. Mind you, the contract was now much more than what the company would have paid if they had asked me to sign before the Olympics. In that meeting, I told Saad that I had been living on Future Life while in London and that I had eaten Future Life a few hours before my historic gold medal win. Paul says:

This was too much for me to hear and I made the call that we must capture this moment in a TV advert. My one concern was that the public might perceive that we were taking advantage of Chad's victory and tagging on our product, and that is why when the advert was screened we had the line, 'This is a true story'.

I have a great relationship with Future Life. The organisation understands my passion for my family, as Paul confirms:

Having met both Chad and Bert, I can see first-hand how important Bert is to Chad. Bert is a good shield of protection, and sometimes to people on the outside their relationship can be misinterpreted, and Bert could be seen as an overprotective and overbearing father. But this is why I believe Chad is also successful, through his dad's positive influence and fathering in all senses of the word. Working with them, I can see that Chad loves and cherishes having his dad around and it's a great example for all of us. We try to promote family values through what we do at Future Life and we believe that Chad is a great ambassador for this. We are really proud of our association with Chad le Clos and wish him well for his prosperous 'future life'. I would like to encourage Chad with these words of encouragement: success is a journey, not a destination.

Future Life's generous support allows me to focus on what I do best – swimming. It is a very successful company. Some say this is because it has developed a great brand, but those who know the company, like me, will testify that it's because they have sound nutritional products that are free from banned substances. The company told me that five out of the six South African gold medallists at London 2012 used Future Life as their main source of nutrition, both in training and before their events.

It's my dream to inspire my fellow South Africans through my swimming. I travel all over the world, but will never trade living in South Africa. I admit that we don't live in a perfect country, but show me a country that doesn't have its fair share of problems. You don't appreciate how fortunate we are in South Africa until you visit other countries.

I have always said that I am proud to be a South African.

9 Chad on Dad

'If I ever stepped out of line, Dad was there to reel me back in.'

I have saved the best for last: now I want to talk about Dad, my hero. Every son looks up to his father, whether his father is aware of it or not. Our relationship goes beyond the usual father–son relationship, as we are like best friends. I can tell Dad almost anything (perhaps not really everything) and we mostly do things together – even if it's just to hit the beach. My father is my biggest fan and supporter, and I am really lucky to have such a close bond with him. He knows what I'm thinking and I allow him to make decisions on my behalf because I trust him and can rely on him to make decisions in my best interest. This relieves me of a lot of pressure and enables me to focus more on my swimming. We understand each other well and he knows what will work best for me.

I think it was only a question of time before my dad was going to become famous. I don't think it had anything to do with luck or coincidence. It was his destiny that one day people would know his name. People who know him realise that his personality is not suited to a life of obscurity. He is bubbly and vivacious and puts people at ease as soon as they meet him. Now nearly everyone knows who Bert le Clos is, and I think there is some truth in it when he jokes that he is more famous than me.

After my victory at the Olympics, when he cheered for me in his deep voice, shouting 'unbelievable', and described me as his 'beautiful boy', it captured the hearts of millions. His 'unbelievable' interview on YouTube registered 600 000 hits in a few hours. The way he comes across in that interview is how he is in real life – that was Dad being himself.

On the back of this popularity he was selected to appear in a TV advertisement singing Nat King Cole's 'Unforgettable', but the song title was replaced with 'Unbelievable'. Dad relishes every moment of this, and when people ask to see the advert, he points to himself on the screen wearing a tuxedo: 'Look at that fat pig.' He jokes about his fame, but it's actually what he has wanted his whole life. At least that's what Mum says. I'm often asked if I feel upstaged by my dad's fame. It can be annoying, I admit. I was once interviewed on CNN and the first thing I was asked was, 'Is your dad here? Can we get him in for a photo?' 'I'm the one who has just won the medals,' I felt like saying. But, no, I don't feel upstaged.

My sister recalls that, as a two-year-old, I did not appear to like Dad very much and cried whenever he came to pick me up from kindergarten. But that soon changed and I used to have daytime naps with my dad from when I was five till around the age of 14. I would place my leg on top of his leg, and if I moved it, he would wake up. I was too embarrassed to tell my friends, but this shows how close we are. Once, when I was about ten, I wanted to go out and play with my friends, so I substituted a cricket bat for my leg because if he had woken up I would have been in trouble. From the age of eight, I remember doing everything with my dad, including surfing.

Dad has taught me and my siblings the value of discipline, and during our upbringing he insisted on us being polite and well mannered, otherwise we were in trouble. These are the basic principles that, sadly, are lacking in some children. At primary school we knew we had to be ready if he was fetching us at a certain time. If I had detention, Dad would be irritated, as it meant I would be late for training. He would politely approach the teacher and explain that he didn't mind if I got punished at lunchtime – but not after school hours, he insisted. Somehow, he managed to get away with it, and even the kids getting a lift with us managed to evade after-school detention.

Dad says that, when I was born, he vowed to Mum that he would make me a champion – probably at soccer. Dad says that in his time he had a good physique and was athletic, but he wasted his talent and gifts. When he used to coach me in soccer, there was one little boy called Michael who had a muscular disorder. He could not run very fast at the practice and could only manage about 4 km/h. Nevertheless, he tried his very best to keep up with the rest. At the end of the session, Dad said, 'Today, the one who trained the hardest was Michael. Well done, you get the chocolate.' I was upset and protested that I had beaten him easily. I will never forget Dad's reply: 'Chad, you did beat him, but you were not running to your full potential and the bottom line is if you want to be a world champion you must give your best all the time. The harder you train, the better you will get. And the more you study, the better marks you will get.'

These words, Dad's positive attitude and his input into my life have helped shape and mould my attitude to life, and my swimming in particular. My life is largely based around my family and it is thanks to my dad that I know how to behave. He has never been averse to correcting me. If I ever stepped out of line, Dad was there to reel me back in. It's easy as a child to develop bad habits, so I am grateful for the discipline he instilled. As I mature, I realise that his approach was because he cared for me. People still compliment me for my manners and behaviour. I have my parents to thank for that.

The other great thing that Dad taught me was never to make excuses. I learnt this lesson when I came second in a juniors race, losing to my friend David Lindeque. At the start of the race I lost my footing slightly, so immediately after the race I said to David that I had slipped and that's the only reason he had beaten me. When Dad heard this, he reprimanded me: 'Chad, you cannot make excuses when you lose. Now apologise to David and his parents.' I did as I was told, and to this day I never make excuses for poor performance. You won't hear me blaming the conditions or circumstances. I do admit that swimming is a sport where the smallest mistakes will cost you, but excuses are not fair – unfair to your opposition and, most importantly, to you.

From what life has taught me thus far, I have learnt the significance of how important the family is. My family is an aspect of my life that I treasure. I love them dearly and cherish each and every one of them. My parents value keeping us together as a family and I enjoy the many times we meet for a meal or go out for a picnic. Family time is very important to me and from the example that Dad sets I know that when I start my own family I will have a great role model to follow.

I appreciate the support I get from my siblings, Bianca, Justin and Jordan. Justin, my elder brother, and his wife Aretha are very supportive and I have learnt a lot from them. They have a little daughter, Riley, whom I love very much. My younger brother, Jordan, is a fiery chap. He is someone you don't want to mess with. He and I have enjoyed each other's company a great deal – playing soccer together in the backyard and our water fights in the pool. Nowadays, I guess he is too busy with the young ladies and doesn't have enough time for me.

Bianca is a great sister to me and someone that I can count on. She helped tremendously to make my 21st party the huge success it was. I adore her kids, my nephews Cruze and Rocco. My brother-in-law, Pedro, has also been like a brother to me since I was about two, which is when he started dating Bianca. Pedro remembers some details of my younger years:

I remember that Chad loved animals. He would ask Bianca, 'Is Pedro an animal people?' If you were not an 'animal people', then he would not take well to you.

I think as part of my induction ritual into the family, Bert used to encourage Chad to hit me. I would often play with Chad (to earn Brownie points with his sister). Bert would have a chat with him and after that he would go ballistic and hit me with sticks. Bert would encourage him: 'Hit harder.' I used to endure it politely and smile. Mind, Chad used to pack a hard whack and one time I remember bleeding, much to the amusement of Bert.

Chad used to love green milkshake. So we used to make this for him, adding green juice for the colour. And there was his 'Mickey pillow'. This was a Mickey Mouse pillow that his grandmother had made for him. If Chad asked for it, you knew it was time for his nap. He would not go to sleep without it.

As he grew up, he loved the Ninja Turtles and playing the *Lion King* video game. Playing it with Chad, I think I got more hooked on it than him. From a young age, Chad was very competitive. I recall teaching him to play eight-ball pool. By the time he was about eight, he was so good at it that he used to beat most of us. He never liked losing and I can remember him also hitting us with the pool cue when we beat him.

Bianca and I went to Dubai in 2010 and saw him win the gold at the World Cup. We were so proud of our 'little Chad'. There is a photo of Bianca and me crying when we saw Chad win the gold medal in London 2012 – that photo made the front page of *The Mercury*. I joke with Chad that I was only crying because I was disappointed that Phelps had lost. Like many others, we initially thought that he had got the silver because the race had been so close. We were so emotionally overwhelmed when we learnt he had won gold that the tears just flowed. We knew how much he had sacrificed and what a great effort he had put in to achieve that gold, so we were beside ourselves with joy. His brother Justin summed up his victory that night quite well: 'He has the heart of a lion. Anyone would have been as nervous as ever seeing Michael Phelps's performance in the semi-final. But Chad focused, this was his dream. He lived his life for this moment and he achieved it.'

We are really proud of Chad and we know that greater things are yet to come from him.

I believe that the family is the basic building block for society. When we consider the communities that we live in, we can see that the family unit is the foundational component upon which any community rests. From strong families we get strong communities and that leads to a great country.

I don't believe that there is any such thing as a perfect family, but I would not trade mine for the world!

I will always think back to the moment I won an Olympic gold on 31 July 2012; I will always remember the Laureus awards; I will always remember the time that Bismarck du Plessis said hello to me at the airport after the World Cup. Learning from such people, I will always try my best, even if it's just to make one fan a day happy – but it's not easy being in the public eye the whole time.

At the pool, if a youngster asks me for a photo, I tell that person, 'Listen, I want to see you in the Olympics in 2020.' That may spur them on and they'll remember those words forever. I feel that there are many things that I should be doing to help those less fortunate than me. My own motivation is to do what I do and do it well. That's why I train so hard and make sacrifices, because I can't inspire people if I am not winning. I have been privileged and seen the world at 21 but I am only kidding myself if I say that Chad le Clos 'has arrived'. I do accept that there are many people who have achieved a lot more than me in life, including people who don't do sport. Recently, at a gala in Durban, I met a woman who gave me a sports massage and when I offered to pay her, she didn't want to take the money. I found out later that she was very poor and couldn't afford to send her child to swimming lessons. I take my hat off to people like that. Through her talent, she wants to make people happy. You don't have to have a certificate, a degree or a gold medal to do some good in the world. It is sound principles that are important.

There's still a lot more I want to do in my sport and in my life. The message behind this book is that I am not resting on what I have achieved so far, because this is not the end. I still have hopes of doing better than I did in London in 2012 – there is still Rio 2016 and beyond. This book is to inspire others through what I have accomplished so far. I believe that the best is still ahead for Chad le Clos and for South Africa. It's a message of hope that I like to share with people everywhere I go. God has given me talent and opportunities, and I want to use these to make a positive difference wherever I go.

I have asked my coach, Graham Hill, to write a few final words at the end of the book. He has been like a second father to me, considering the amount of time we spend together. He is a tough disciplinarian and he pushes me to the limit. This is what makes Graham so good. We have a very close relationship and I admire and respect him a lot. There is a lot that I could say about my training and preparation, but I think Graham can provide better insight. I have asked Graham to be as candid as possible: we have no secrets about our success, and we both believe that there are no short cuts to achieving it. You will also see why I say that Graham pushes me to the limits.

I look forward to hearing from you about what you think about my first book. You can catch me on Facebook or Twitter.

Coach Graham Hill on Chad's goals for his future in swimming

'I believe that whatever you put into the programme is what you are going to get out.'

In writing these closing words, let me expand on some of my earlier comments in the book. Chad has asked me to be as candid as possible, so I will share with you the details of our plan and its execution towards 'world domination'. World domination in swimming, that is! I have trained many talented swimmers in my coaching career, but what sets Chad apart from the rest is his great attitude. And this positive attitude begins at training. Let me explain.

The gutter

In the training pool, we refer to the lane next to the wall as 'the gutter'. In that lane are the pumps for the pool, so when you are in the gutter, you have to swim against a current. Everyone in the club has to have their turn in the gutter and if someone complains about it, I ask Chad to go into that lane. He always obliges despite being the Olympic champion, such is his humility.

At training Chad doesn't have his own lane to himself: he trains like the other swimmers, with two or three in the same lane.

Breaststroke before butterfly

When I first began working with Chad, he wasn't really a butterfly swimmer. It was his breaststroke that was exceptional. I thought he would do well at the IM, as he had a killer breaststroke and he was pretty decent in the other three strokes too. In his early days, he used to swim phenomenal times in breaststroke, but then he got injured. That injury cost him a lot of success at the breaststroke. I was devastated by his injury, as I had coached Terence Parkin to silver in the Olympics and thought that Chad had the potential to be the next breaststroke champion. And with a powerful breaststroke, Chad would have also been a great contender for the IM gold.

After his injury, though, the butterfly became his strongest stroke, and after he was captivated by Michael Phelps's performance in the 2004 Athens Olympics, Chad wanted to swim the butterfly. Butterfly is a more demanding stroke. It requires more than just power – it also demands timing and the right feel and body movement. Power does matter, but along with the swimmer's movement, the timing has to be spot on and in sync.

The team

It's not an easy road to being a champion. A lot of people watch the Games on TV and say to themselves, 'I wish I could do what they do.' But what happens behind the scenes is what really counts. That's the hard part of the whole journey. I like to refer to it as 'from Olympic gold medals to becoming princesses'. (I also coached Charlene Wittstock, now Princess Charlene of Monaco.)

This journey is not just about me, the coach, and Chad, the swimmer: it requires a team effort. As we reached the top levels, it was evident that everyone wanted a piece of Chad. People we had never seen before – VIPs and dignitaries – were now at the poolside. We had been competing for the past 12 years and had never seen them before, but you have to expect that when you hit the big time.

Chad is the one who does all the hard work, but he also has to be surrounded by the best. He needs the support of his family, the South African Sports Confederation and Olympic Committee (SASCOC), the physio, the team doctors and the moral support of his teammates. My role in this team is rather like that of a CEO, as I am heavily involved in the planning, which cannot be done without the support of other key role players. Ask any top international sportsperson and they will confirm that their success can't be achieved without a support team being in place.

Thus far, the most rewarding part of my career has been the London 2012 Olympics. What made it more special was Chad beating Michael Phelps, a legend in the world of sport and the most decorated swimmer of all time. And, as you know, he was also Chad's hero from a young age.

Preparation is key

As part of our preparation for the Olympics, it was important that we raced as many times as we could against the best. So, before the Olympics, we were away from home for about three months. Those competitions were very important in preparing Chad for London 2012. Racing against the best before the Olympics had a calming effect because the opposition were not strangers any more to Chad. The downside is that it's very taxing being away from your family for a long time, but that is something that comes with the territory.

I was looking for continuous, consistent performance from Chad. When we toured Europe for the three months before the Olympics we aimed for a race time of 1.55 for the 200 m butterfly, which was around Chad's best time. During that period, we were doing intensive training – about 16 to 18 km a day. During competitions, this drops to around 10 km a day. And if we could do this and beat the opposition in the run-up to the Olympics, I knew that we had a good chance of beating Michael Phelps. I didn't stick to the same training routine, but used to mix it up a bit to find out what worked best.

Success is not about being lucky on the day. It comes down to thorough preparation. I can claim that, contrary to what some people think, we did not beat Michael Phelps out of luck: it was the result of planning and properly executing the plan.

Knowing your opposition

In 2009, at Chad's first FINA-Arena Swimming World Cup in Berlin, he sent me a message saying that he was racing alongside Michael Phelps, in the lane next to him. Phelps had recently won eight gold medals at the 2008 Beijing Olympics, so it was quite a big thing for Chad, a 16-year-old, to be lined up against the world leader, especially since he was Chad's hero.

I always tried to get to know who our opposition would be, and Phelps was up there as the main opponent. Chad had also made it clear that he wanted to beat him. I like to learn about the opposition, to understand their tactics. This is crucial for race preparation. I like to read their body language and pick up their habits before a race – like poker players analysing one other. I would survey swimmers like Phelps and Matsuda when I attended galas. Some people thought it was bizarre the way I studied them to establish if they were still fresh and to discern what they were thinking, but one can learn a lot from this exercise.

At the Youth Olympics in Singapore, when I saw what Chad could do when he brought home five medals (including a gold), I was confident he could do well in the Commonwealth Games in Delhi and would pose a threat to the seniors. The secret was we did not rest, shave (front, back and everywhere) or taper Chad (which means being fully rested going into a competition). I wanted to see how Chad performed 'raw', without these accepted, performance-enhancing practices. The reality of competitive swimming is that every millisecond counts, which is why such practices are the norm. However, as Chad's potential was still not fully realised, we chose not to reveal to our opposition too much of what Chad was capable of, so I chose not to do all of them at once. In Delhi I was confident that Chad was going to break into the international scene at the Commonwealth Games, which was the big one for us in 2010.

I rested him for Delhi and he went into the Singapore event unshaved – in a sense, keeping some of his potential in reserve. In Delhi he won two gold medals and showed the world he could be the best and compete with the best. I believe that whatever you put into the programme is what you are going to get out. I believe strongly in this theory: if you don't put in the hard work, you are not going to get anything good out of it.

I knew that when Chad is rested and shaved, he could swim at close to his best training times and I knew bigger things would come when I rested him. Even with the injury, Chad still did well at the 2010 Commonwealth Games and the 2011 World Championships. He was carrying that injury till at least March 2012. It didn't heal well, as he did not have sufficient time for rest and treatment, largely because of his gruelling programme. It was a formidable achievement for Chad to become Commonwealth champion and world champion with an injured groin. And his butterfly was getting better all the time as we worked harder on it.

What he did in 2010 at the Commonwealth Games showed me he had the potential for greater achievements. After the Commonwealth Games, Chad was excited and said to me, 'I want to get a medal in the 2011 World Champs.'

This was less than ten months away, so I told him, 'Slow down. Let's just get to the finals and finish in the top five. That would be absolutely fine.' He ended up finishing fifth, which I felt was great. However, once I watched the replay of the race, I was upset because I noticed that he had had a bad last turn. Wu Peng was able to swim faster and finished third, which Chad could easily have managed had he done a better last turn.

I have always been telling coaches around the world to watch this boy. I even pointed him out to Bob Bowman, Michael Phelps's coach, at the Rome World Championships in 2009. After the 200 m butterfly heats, when Michael Phelps and Chad were loosening down in the indoor pool, I said to Bowman, 'That's my guy who just swam the 200 m butterfly.' I introduced Chad to Bowman, who asked Chad what time he had swum. Chad said that he had missed out by 0.09 seconds, but Bob wanted to know his time, so Chad told him: 156.90. Bowman was impressed, but it probably did not matter much to him, as Chad's achievements were not significant enough to threaten Team Phelps.

I really wanted Chad to swim faster in the heats, but at the time it seemed as if he didn't listen. To drive home this point, in the 400 m IM heats I shouted for the other guys to swim faster so that they could beat Chad's time and he would miss out on the finals. I was prepared to spur on the others to teach Chad a lesson. This tough approach surprised the other swimmers.

Chad made the finals at the Rome 2009 World Championships in lane 8 and got the silver, behind Thiago Pereira, the winner. It was a good result, but, more importantly, he learnt what I was trying to teach him: that he had to swim his best in the heats or there would be no final for him.

In the Short-Course World Cup 2011 in Japan, in the final leg Chad was leading the series. Going into the last day, we were very tired as we had been travelling a great deal. After the heats, I suggested to Chad that it might be a better idea to sleep at the stadium rather than returning to the hotel. We were exhausted and it made sense, as we had to be back at the pool early the next morning. So we slept at the pool in a corridor.

The next day, Chad won the 200 m freestyle and that was enough for him to win the overall series.

Underplaying Chad's potential

Chad has asked me to share a brief overview of our plan to win the gold and defeat Phelps. It was all about planning, and in the South African team we planned to win two medals and beat Phelps. SASCOC asked a hard question: 'How many medals can we expect and how will Team South Africa feature?' At times I had to be a politician, but I couldn't over promise because if we didn't deliver I would have to answer for it. So, my strategy was to underplay our potential, and the one team member I underplayed a lot was Chad. I don't think he realised it. I spoke to SASCOC about Cameron van der Burgh, as he was a seasoned campaigner, the number-one seed in the world and the current world-record holder. Being a world champion, Cameron was the obvious favourite for us to get a gold. I didn't want to pressurise Cameron, but everyone was expecting him to bring home the gold. We were also banking on the 4 x 100 m medley relay.

Quietly on the side, however, I was expecting Chad to pull off one of the greatest surprises by beating Michael Phelps. An important part of our preparation was getting buy-in from the South African Swimming Federation for funding, as we needed to travel the world to race and prepare. During the 24-month period preceding the 2012 London Olympics, I really believed we had a chance of beating Phelps. I don't think Phelps or his coach even knew who Chad was 24 months before the 2012 Olympics.

The pep talk

Moments before Chad went to report to the call room, before the start of the 200 m butterfly final, he approached me. He asked me if I had any last words of advice. We had prepared enough and I was not going to go over the game plan again, so I just wanted to say something that would spark him up: 'This is the last time you will ever get to race Michael Phelps in the 200 m butterfly. If you want to beat him, you have to beat him tonight. This is your last chance,' I said.

The game plan

Our plan was, from the heats and the semi-finals, to get a position in the middle of the pool. Phelps always swam a hard heat in order to get a good lane placing, so I am glad that Chad listened and stuck to our game plan and swam well in the heats. Going into finals, he had a faster time than Phelps.

For the final, our game plan was not to lead the race: we were going to swim off Michael Phelps, as we knew that if we wanted to win, we had to adopt this tactic. We knew what pace Michael Phelps was going to set, so I prepared Chad for it and the plan was for him to stick right on Phelps's shoulder. We had observed that Phelps does put in a little more effort on the third length, creating more distance between himself and the others. Phelps couldn't accelerate over the final lap. Working with sports scientists and looking at video footages over the years, we had picked up that, over the last 50 m, when Phelps tends to destroy the rest of the field, he keeps a constant speed. Chad, however, can produce good acceleration. Therefore, if Chad could stay with him, he could overtake Phelps at the end. I didn't expect it to be that close: it was fingernails.

By the final turn, if anyone is still close to him, Phelps blows them away with his underwater work. So Chad and I went over this religiously so that he knew how important it was for him to sit with Phelps until that crucial final turn. We had worked really hard to be there for the last 50 m. To prepare for that final turn, we worked on Chad's underwaters. This proved to have been good preparation, as Chad executed a perfect final turn. When he came out of the final turn, he was right there with Michael Phelps, on his shoulder. He then produced the speed to swim 'over the top' of Phelps, to produce one of the biggest upsets of the Olympic Games.

People think that I would have been nervous watching that race as the coach, but in reality I was relaxed because it was the one time that Chad had swum a race of pure perfection. And it needed to be if he was going to win the Olympic final. Chad also said that he felt relaxed before the race – I pointed out that this was because he had already done the work and was therefore prepared.

After he won the 200 m butterfly, I was confident Chad could also win the 100 m butterfly, so I scratched him from the 200 m IM after he had qualified for that final. In theory, I wanted to keep his mind off the 100 m butterfly, so I made him swim the heats and semis. I believed he could win. After watching the replay of the 100 m butterfly final, I noticed that he had too much hang time on the walls and was slightly slow on the wall. The difference between Chad and Phelps was 0.2 seconds; Chad took the silver.

Self-belief

Chad had immense hunger and determination to beat Michael Phelps and he believed that he could do it. In our training sets and programmes, I reinforced this self-belief and instilled in him the confidence that he could do it. Chad knew everything there was to know about Michael

Phelps. He probably knew Phelps better than Phelps did himself in terms of his achievements and statistics. I designed his training programmes around that information.

The self-belief, passion and hard work that had gone into the preparation explain why Chad was so emotional on the Olympic podium. I knew what was going through his mind: he was thinking of the sacrifices everyone had made to help him get there – that was the passion coming out. I joke and say that, in our 14 years together, that race was the first time Chad had listened to me 100 per cent. It culminated in the perfect race.

Chad said before the 200 m butterfly final that he experienced no nerves. The reason we were both so relaxed was that, if you plan it correctly and you have the goods to work with, you can achieve anything.

Graham Hill

Writer's note

Having spent a lot of time with Chad and his family and friends, I can say that it's not just the medals that make him the 'golden boy' – but his heart too. Chad has a heart of gold. His humility and care for others, even complete strangers, is commendable. He always has a smile and an encouraging word to share with everyone.

His commitment to pursuing his dream is an inspiration to us all. His is a story that I hope will encourage many others to believe that nothing is impossible if you put in the hard work. I have seen the dedication and sacrifices that Chad and his parents have made to help him achieve all that he has, so I can confidently say that great sacrifice always precedes great results.

It is Chad's hope that this book will serve as an inspiration to others, that they should never give up on their dreams, no matter how big or 'unbelievable' they may be. He has been honest in sharing with me what it took to beat the world's greatest swimmer, Michael Phelps, at the 2012 Olympics and I believe that this book will do just that – help others achieve the unbelievable.

Myan Subrayan

Acknowledgements from Chad

My thanks must first go to my parents. You have never let me down and everything you have done has been to accommodate my needs. This has meant you've made many sacrifices to help my dream become a reality, and this thanks also goes to my siblings: Bianca, Justin, Jordan, and their respective families as well.

To Sam Ramsamy, for championing the cause of sports in South Africa and ensuring we were able to get back to competing on the international scene. Thank you especially for taking the time to pen the foreword to this book, and also for your continued support and encouragement of me as I compete locally and abroad.

To my coach, mentor and friend, Graham Hill. Thanks for your contributions and for writing about our plans for my future in swimming in this book. We have been together for almost 14 years and I am truly grateful for your wisdom and valuable input in your support of my swimming journey. It has been great so far, but I know the best is yet to come!

To all my friends and family: knowing that I have your support is a big help and comfort to me. I love you guys. I'm sorry that I can't mention you all by name, but that would take ages! Thank you as well to those who gave special contributions in this book.

To my sponsors: Arena, Omega, Future Life and Volkswagen. Thank you for partnering with me. Your support is a huge help and is much appreciated.

To my fans and supporters for sticking by me all the way: always know that your support is invaluable and I appreciate it very much. I may not have time to respond to all your Facebook and Twitter comments, but know that I do read them. Keep them coming!

Special thanks to my writer, Myan Subrayan, who has made the book that you hold in your hands possible. Your time and effort, which has included many trips to Durban to meet with me and my family, has been special. You are more than just my writer – you have become a friend to the Le Clos family. Thanks as well to your wife, Jolene, and your lovely girls.

My thanks would not be complete if I did not acknowledge and thank God for my family and the talent and ability He has given me.

References

The East German Doping Machine. (2006). Retrieved from International Swimming Hall of Fame: http://www.ishof.org/Honorees/german_doping.htm

Commonwealth Games and Olympic Youth Champion Chad le Clos Signs Sponsorship Deal with Arena. (2010, October 7). Retrieved from Arena: http://arenaitalia.it/News.aspx?prd=366&lng=0

CHAD LE CLOS WILL BE "SWIMMING FOR CANSA" IN STOCKHOLM LEG OF FINA/ARENA WORLD CUP. (2011, October 14). Retrieved from Arena: http://www.arenainternational.com/chad-le-clos-will-be-swimming-for-cansa-in-stockholm-leg-of-fina/arena-world-cup_en_0_2_1235.html

Princess Charlene Cheers South Africa to Victory. (2012, August 8). Retrieved from Mad for Monaco: http://madmonaco.blogspot.com/2012/08/princess-charlene-cheers-south-africa.html

Doping in China. (2013, April 16). Retrieved from Wikipedia: http://en.wikipedia.org/wiki/Doping_in_China

Crouse, K. (2009, July 24). *Swimming Bans High-Tech Suits, Ending an Era*. Retrieved from NYTimes.com: http://www.nytimes.com/2009/07/25/sports/25swim.html

Dillman, L. (2009, July 25). *FINA bans bodysuits that have led to spate of world records*. Retrieved from Los Angeles Times: http://articles.latimes.com/2009/jul/25/sports/sp-world-swimming25

Elite Team/Chad le Clos. (2014). Retrieved from Arena: http://www.arenainternational.com/athletes/chad-le-clos_en_0_4_954. html

Hanson, I. (2011, July 14). *USA Swim Team Camp In Australia: Michael Phelps Says World Records Will Fall In Shanghai*. Retrieved from Swimming World Total Access: http://www.swimmingworldmagazine.com/lane9/news/27531.asp

Hart, S. (2009, July 18). *Rebecca Adlington boycotts go-faster swimsuit*. Retrieved from The Telegraph: http://www.telegraph.co.uk/sport/olympics/swimming/5859667/Rebecca-Adlington-boycotts-go-faster-swimsuit.html

Hi-tech suits banned from January. (2009, July 31). Retrieved from BBC Sport: http://news.bbc.co.uk/sport2/hi/other_sports/swimming/8161867.stm

Lambley, G. (2012, July 31). *Chad to add to SA medal tally?* Retrieved from 24.com: http://www.sport24.co.za/OtherSport/Olympics2012/Chad-to-add-to-SA-medal-tally-20120731

McCallum, K. (2012, August 2). *Chad hasn't taken medal off since his win*. Retrieved from IOL News: http://www.iol.co.za/pretoria-news/chad-hasn-t-taken-medal-off-since-his-win-1.1355101#.Uw392_mSySp

Moolla, Y. (2012, August 1). *Family overjoyed by Chad's golden moment*. Retrieved from IOL News: http://www.iol.co.za/news/south-africa/kwazulu-natal/

family-overjoyed-by-chad-s-golden-moment-1.1353728#.Uw323_mSySp

Paine, C. (2012, August 1). *Unbelievable! Chad le Clos's dad is the proudest man at the Games*. Retrieved from The Advertiser: http://www.adelaidenow.com.au/sport/unbelievable-meet-the-proudest-dad-at-the-games/story-fn9dh-vy9-1226440404215

SA's first gold. (2010, October 5). Retrieved from Sowetan Live: http://www.sowetanlive.co.za/sport/2010/10/05/sa_s-first-gold

sport24. (2012, July 29). *Le Clos: Learning curve for me*. Retrieved from 24.com: http://www.sport24.co.za/OtherSport/Olympics2012/Le-Clos-Learning-curve-for-me-20120729

sport24. (2012, August 1). *Phelps praises Le Clos*. Retrieved from 24.com: http://www.sport24.co.za/OtherSport/Olympics2012/Phelps-praises-Le-Clos-20120801

sport24. (2012, August 4). *Phelps 'watching' Le Clos*. Retrieved from 24.com: http://www.sport24.co.za/OtherSport/Olympics2012/Phelps-watching-Le-Clos-20120804

sport24. (2012, May 10). *Road to London: Chad le Clos*. Retrieved from 24.com: http://www.sport24.co.za/OtherSport/Road-to-London-Chad-le-Clos-20120510

watchSportNews. (2012, August 6). *London 2012: MICHAEL PHELPS official VISA Press Conference*. Retrieved from Youtube: http://www.youtube.com/watch?v=OqZM2DO-jAE

Yocom, G. (2002, October). *My Shot: Gary Player*. Retrieved from Golf Digest: http://www.golfdigest.com/magazine/myshot_gd0210